Jackie Chan

JACKIE CHAN

INSIDE THE DRAGON

Clyde Gentry III

Taylor Publishing Company

Dallas, Texas

Published by Taylor Publishing Company
1550 West Mockingbird Lane
Dallas, Texas 75235
www.taylorpub.com

Designed by David Timmons

Portions of the interviews with Jackie Chan have previously been published in *Hong Kong Film Connection.*

Frontispiece photograph from *Mr. Nice Guy* courtesy Golden Harvest.

The publisher would like to thank Sara Urquidez for the photographs of Benny Urquidez and Jackie Chan. Comic book art © 1997 Jackie & Willie Productions, Ltd. Published exclusively by The Topps Company.

This book is not authorized by Jackie Chan or Jackie & Willie Productions, Ltd.

Library of Congress Cataloging-in-Publication Data

        Gentry, Clyde
           Jackie Chan : inside the dragon / Clyde Gentry III.
                p.   cm.
           Filmography: p.
           Includes bibliographical references and index.
           ISBN 0-87833-962-0 (pbk.)
           1. Ch'eng, Lung, 1955– . I. Title.
        PN2878.C52G46 1997
        791.43'028'092—dc21

                                     97-5906
                                     CIP

Printed in the United States of America

10 9 8 7 6 5 4 3 2 1

Contents

Preface

It's hard to believe that Jackie Chan—who has won the world over with his unique approach to filmmaking—has never been the subject of a book. While this book can't possibly cover every aspect of his cinematic life, I hope that readers will come away appreciating Jackie Chan more. Here is an introduction to what his films are about, who he has worked with, and how his films are made. Chan's career and life are multi-faceted, so, rather than approaching Chan's story simply chronologically, I have given each facet—each theme—its own chapter. To make this book as comprehensive as possible, I briefly discuss many of his martial arts and filmmaking techniques since both of these aspects have attracted fans who may not be Hong Kong film fans by nature.

All of the films discussed are the original, full-length Chinese versions. Where it is necessary, I mention other versions, but the originally released films are the ones I base my discussions on. Many of the English versions floating around are not complete and the dubbing often changes the meaning of what was actually said in the film.

I have also included the Chinese characters for the names Chan and many of the people he has worked with in the past with an explanation of how understanding these names will help in your quest for Chan's films (and others discussed here) in Chinese video stores.

Everything in this book is based on many interviews conducted with Jackie Chan and the people who know him best. I hope this book answers many of your questions and leads to other books written on the man of the hour.

✳

Special Thanks

Special acknowledgment must go to Edward Tang for his patience in answering hours of questions about the many of Chan's best films.

Thanks to Ng See-yuen, Chua Lam, Hal Needham, Gary Daniels, Richard Norton, Benny and Sara Urquidez, Whang Inn-sik, Keith Vitali, Mars, Tai Po, Roberta Chow, Stanley Tong, Ric Meyers, Alan Sit, Marc Akerstream, Shu Kei, Richard Ng, Sammo Hung, Kenneth Low, Russell Cawthorne, Willie Chan, Elliot Tong, Michael Stradford, Joy Al-Sofi, Stuart Sobel, Renee Witterstaetter, Cynthia Rothrock, Colin Geddes, John Marsh, John Gainfort, Jim Donovan, Ronald Ng, John Nicholas, Joey O'Bryan, Mi Mi Lai, Wilson Yu, Damon Foster, David Zeve, Barrie Pattison, Mable Chan, Ricky Miller, James Ha, Kelly Stone, Lee Rebouche, Winnie Chan of Golden Harvest, and Bey Logan and Media Asia Group.

Translations, Chinese interviews, and lessons in Chinese protocol supplied by Sam Ho, Lei Wei, and Lily Chiang. I am eternally grateful.

From Taylor Publishing Company: Holly McGuire, Heather Hitchcock, and a dedicated staff.

Dedicated to my family and friends who all thought my addiction to Hong Kong cinema was crazy. Has anything changed?

And to Jackie Chan: my love for Hong Kong cinema started with your films and you have kept that interst growing for many years.

They Call Me Bruce?

"Bruce Lee number one. John Wayne number two. Jackie Chan number three. That's the way I would like to be remembered in the history books."

—*Jackie Chan*

Not since the death of Bruce Lee in 1973 has the world claimed a cinematic icon greater than Jackie Chan. While Hollywood creates lethargic, pretentious productions starring multimillion-dollar actors, Chan's vision has remained pure and simple despite temptation. That vision is forged from the comic inventiveness of the silent era, the traditionalism of the East, and the basic semantics of the common man. Chan has escaped the unpopular label of "Bruce Lee imitator" to become an international phenomenon claiming legions of fans around the globe and transcending cultural boundaries. Chan has kept the entire Hong Kong film industry afloat for two decades, sustaining the interest of foreign investors and distributors despite the decreasing quality of Hong Kong films in general. And yet, with more than forty starring roles under his belt, Jackie Chan's ultimate love is unchanged: to bring "something different" to the screen each time.

In the end, audiences are treated to an awe-inspiring experience much like watching acrobats on the trapeze, though Chan's inventive action sequences go far beyond any circus act. He doesn't require the new technologies of Hollywood special effects or even a well-written script. He *is* the special effect. Chan has created his own genre, one that enables him to play his underdog hero in every film without letting his audience grow tired of a routine. He shapes his inventions by exerting firm control over every facet of film production, building an impressive career as a stuntman, actor, director, producer, choreographer, writer, and singer in the process. Now, having gained

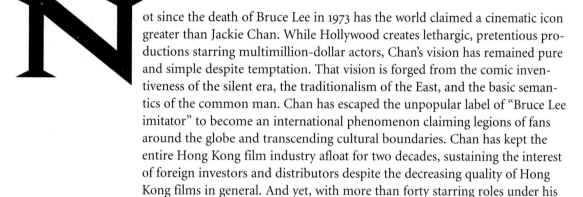

Half a Loaf of Kung Fu (1978). (*Colin Geddes/Asian Eye*)

the recognition of American audiences, Chan has transcended cultural (and cultish) pigeon-holing: he is no longer the "Clown Prince of Kung Fu."

Audiences haven't seen a screen character like Jackie Chan for more than sixty years. With Charlie Chaplin's accented facial mannerisms, Buster Keaton's unpredictable physical feats, and Fred Astaire's rhythm in gliding across the screen, Chan can be enjoyed universally by all who miss the innocent romance with the camera that has been lost in present-day Hollywood stylizations. Let this book serve as well-deserved fanfare of his storybook rise to fame, exploring the components of his charmingly guileless on-screen presence, the films that made him a success, and his breathtaking filmmaking techniques—especially his world-renowned action sequences.

Jackie Chan was born in Hong Kong on April 7, 1954, as Jacky Chan Kong-sang to Charles and Lee Lee Chan, a cook and a cleaning lady, respectively. Born to poverty-stricken parents, Chan was almost sold for a mere $26 to the British doctor who delivered him. Charles Chan, skilled in the martial arts, began pushing Jacky at an early age into athletics. The young Chan would wake up at six in the morning to commence training: a quick jog, then a workout on wooden shelves and sandbags made up by his father. The young Chan was more interested in playing games than studying, so his father had to find an outlet for his son's energy. With little money to care for Jacky and aspirations to work for the American embassy in Australia (Charles was the personal cook for the Australian consulate), Charles eventually took Jacky to Zhonggou Xiju Xueyan (Chinese Opera Research Institute) in Hong Kong at the age of seven and a half. The institute was located in Tsimshatsui, a thriving district in Kowloon where Chan's offices stand today. With only 1,900 square feet to work with, the institute was unusually small for a drama academy of this type. Still, the school's headmaster, Yu Jim-yuen, more than made up for the lack of size. There

were several instructors, but Yu was the driving force behind the success of its students. The young Chan signed a seven-year apprenticeship contract here in 1961, although he would follow Yu for another three years.

Chinese Opera dates back many centuries to the Southern and Northern dynasties, when ancient songs and dances were offered to the gods for good fortune. As it evolved, the operas examined human mores, drawing from Chinese history and folklore and using music to drive the action. The operas are a pageant of color, song, and action. Although every region had its own style of opera, Peking Opera became the paradigm, bringing together, in fact, other regional operas. Now, the terms *Peking Opera* and *Chinese Opera* are used interchangeably.

To be a Chinese Opera performer demanded abilities in dancing, singing, acrobatics, martial arts, and stage makeup. As author Tyan Shuh-lin explains in *How To Appreciate Chinese Opera,* "The movements of Chinese Opera not only call for grace in posing, but also for meticulous coordination with the pace set by the beat of the drums and agreement with the nature of the music."

To meet the demand for performers, Chinese Opera schools sprang up everywhere across China. And because the performers had to have incredible physical abilities, children were recruited who could undergo intense training. Essentially traveling circuses, Peking Opera schools served as pseudo-foster homes for many children whose parents couldn't afford to keep them. Out of respect for the headmaster, the students would assume names as part of his family, so Yu Jim-yuen's name was incorporated into those of his students. Here, Yuen Lau (as Chan was named) would work from 5 a.m. to midnight with the other students, learning every aspect of stage performance, including stage makeup application and acting. Chan was the mischievous one of the group and was more regarded for his singing ability than for his martial arts skills.

At the Chinese Opera Research Institute, the children had to sign waivers giving the teachers full control to use whatever means necessary to (sometimes literally) whip them into shape. The students also signed contracts stating that whatever money they made performing would go to the master and that parents were not allowed to watch their own children learning. The students would be taught many different drills to prepare them for the stage: waist and foot training (an exercise for balance and coordination), circle running, broken-step walk (a term that describes simple stances and movements for martial arts), and types of wrestling. Instead of grades, food would be the reward for completing these tasks, and the master had no problem using his thick whip to exert power. At the end of each night, the students would have to serve their master through a variety of massaging techniques—bringing the master's strength back, ironically, for tomorrow's punishment.

It was here that Chan, affectionately called "Big Nose," befriended many students who would eventually grow up with him and become big stars on their own. Sammo Hung Kam-bo (Chu Yuen Lung), Yuen Biao, Yuen Kwai, and Yuen Wah were some of them. With Chan, they formed the Seven Little Fortunes Opera group. The group actually had fourteen members, but only seven would appear on stage at one time. Chan's father came to visit his son once every two years until his unsuccessful business in Australia kept him from doing so. Chan's parents would keep in contact with him almost entirely by mail, managing to send him some money each month, but his real family was his teacher and his schoolmates (whom he claimed as his "brothers").

Performing live gave these youngsters a chance to exercise their skills, but the early six-

A scene from *Painted Faces*, a film based on the Seven Little Fortune's experiences in the Chinese Opera Research Institute.

In 1989 a rare collaboration between Golden Harvest and the Shaw Brothers created *Painted Faces*, a film based on the life and times of Jackie and his fellow Peking Opera school friends. Sammo Hung played the role of Master Yu Jim-yuen, and Yuen Wah choreographed the film. Chan himself is quick to mention that the film is actually only 20% accurate. He likens *his* experience to that depicted in the popular Chinese film *Farewell My Concubine* (1993). Sammo Hung was quoted as saying that the exercises performed in *Painted Faces* were actually the exercises that the real Mr. Yu practiced when he was a student at a similar school. Master Yu did attend the film's premiere in Hong Kong. "[He] didn't like it or my performance very much," recalled Hung recently. "He said that he was portrayed as being too stern when actually he was much, much worse!" Master Yu presently resides in Los Angeles but has Alzheimer's disease—he didn't even recognize Chan when he came to visit him.

Bruce Lee in *Enter the Dragon* **(1973).**

ties brought the deterioration of Peking Opera. Burlesque shows and the cinema were becoming more popular. Chan and his new family had to keep working, so they moved to films. In 1962, one year after his induction into the Peking Opera school, Chan made his film debut in *Big and Little Wong Tin Bar*, one of several childhood films he called "seven-day films" because they would take only seven days to shoot.

By 1971, Chan (who was seventeen) and his Peking Opera school chums were out of luck. The school closed down, leaving its uneducated students (reading and writing were secondary skills) to fend for themselves. They had vast stage knowledge, but Cantonese opera films were meeting a fate similar to that of the stage productions. Musicals and films with anti-Japanese themes were beginning to decline, as well, so breaking into kung fu films was their only choice. Wu xia pian (Cantonese martial arts) was becoming one of the most important Cantonese film genres at the time. The films were nothing more than longer, less arty versions of Peking Opera, so it was a natural progression for the students to find cinema work as bit players and stuntmen. The popularity of Chinese kung fu films was not unlike America's

fascination with movies about the Old West. While America had Billy the Kid and other legendary gunslingers, Chinese historical figures, such as Hwang Fei-hung, became bigger than life on the screen. Instead of guns and plots dealing with families fighting over land, it was kung fu and martial arts clans fighting over supremacy of styles. Even though the genre was limited in terms of sets and plots, the films could be made in weeks, and scripts could be watered down since the films were mostly fighting.

When the Shaw Brothers film studio released *The One-Armed Swordsman* in 1968, it was a transitional sign that something was about to change in the realm of the martial arts film genre. As Ric Meyers, author of *From Bruce Lee to the Ninjas*, explains, "After years of Confucian morality and bloodless, unconvincing, stagy fights, *The One-Armed Swordsman* showed them a tortured anti-hero who thought nothing of slaughtering his enemies." The film launched director Chang Cheh as the master of kung fu/swordplay mayhem, but the real significance of this film is how it paved the way for the new screen hero who was about to dominate the industry.

When Bruce Lee leapt off the screen in *Fists of Fury* (the Hong Kong title is *The Big Boss*)[1] in 1971, he literally destroyed the fancier, stagelike martial arts productions and replaced them with a realism that the genre had been lacking. The difference between Lee and *One-Armed Swordsman* star Wang Yu was simple: Lee was an unrelenting and unbeatable hero.

Lee personified the heart and soul of why this genre was important, and the unemployed Peking Opera graduates had no problem assimilating. Yuen Wah found the most significant role

---

[1] American release titles are used here, with the original Hong Kong titles in parentheses—since these titles are what can be found through video outlets. The alternate titles of Lee's films can be confusing: what was *The Big Boss* in Hong Kong became *Fists of Fury* in America, while *Fist of Fury* was retitled *The Chinese Connection*.

as Bruce Lee's stunt double, performing all of the acrobatic needs of Lee's roles. Yuen can be seen in *The Chinese Connection* (*Fist of Fury*) as a Japanese student who mocks Lee as he approaches the gate with its famous inscription "No Chinese or Dogs Allowed." Jackie Chan appears in a brief shot at the beginning of *The Chinese Connection* and also worked as a stunt-man on the film (he doubled for Mr. Suzuki, who is kicked through the wall during the final fight). Chan was one of many oncomers who attack Lee in Han's underground headquarters in *Enter the Dragon*: Chan bear hugs Lee only to have Lee grab him by the hair and snap his neck. Sammo Hung fought Lee at the beginning of *Enter the Dragon* and even served as second unit director and bit player on *Game of Death*.

Up until this time in Hong Kong cinema, screen presence was not an essential aspect of an actor's performance. Films were shot in very short time periods, and actors didn't have to worry about diction since Chinese dialects other than Cantonese (Hong Kong's main dialect) were dubbed in. The explanation for this dubbing is complex. Cantonese opera films did display an actor's vocal potential, since they were shot in synch-sound for Hong Kong audiences only, but for other Chinese films, it was important for actors to be able to speak in impeccable Mandarin—the language of 90% of China's population—which not all actors could do. As a result, it was necessary to shoot the films silently. Then the film would be dubbed into Cantonese or Mandarin using only native speakers in those languages—actors often didn't dub their own voices. (A jolly man named Chan Bo-wing actually made a career out of dubbing the Cantonese voices for Jackie Chan and Sammo Hung.) So synch-sound filmmaking—where sound and action are recorded/filmed at the same time—was abolished. This practice was carried on for nearly three decades, until director Stanley Tong insisted on synch-sound in *Police Story III: Super Cop* in 1992. Several directors followed suit shortly thereafter, using Cantonese as the central dialect for the films.

As for Bruce Lee, his on-screen persona came from the soul. He brought his unrelenting powerfulness to the screen the same way he brought it to the streets of Hong Kong. In all five of his feature films, Lee's on-screen persona, accented by his unique mannerisms, is unmistakable to the audience. If anything, Lee and Chan shared a need to establish a hero with whom the audience could easily identify. For Lee, it was the energized, stifled mannequin hero who blurted out the high-pitched "key-ops!" and grimaced at the camera with serious conviction.

Bruce Lee was a brooding controller, much like his on-screen persona. He knew what could make him a star on the screen, and he had no problem letting everyone know it. As a tough kid growing up in Hong Kong, Lee's approach was "my way." Period. After moving from secondary lead to star in *Fists of Fury*, Lee didn't have to explain anything to the producers. He merely took charge of each project and acted accordingly. With prosperous box office receipts, no one complained.

As Jackie Chan's career began to materialize, his on-screen persona distanced itself from Lee's. It took almost ten years and ten films for this transformation. Many people still believe that Chan is still just a Lee imitator, but nothing could be further from the truth once Chan was able to get the same kind of control that Lee had over his productions.

It was a painful time indeed for Chan, and Master Yu's training was just a precursor to the repetitive adversity that he would face. Whereas Sammo Hung became an understudy for Huang Feng, one of Hong Kong's most celebrated action directors, and found work as a villain despite his portly figure, Jackie Chan couldn't find anything to really suit him. In 1971, on the recommendation of an older classmate (actually the only girl in the group), Chan landed his first starring role (using his new name, Chan Yuen Lung) in the *Young Tiger of Canton*, but it was shelved and left uncompleted. Years later it would be released as *Master with Cracked Fingers* (among other titles), boasting extra scenes with a Chan look-alike. In 1973, Chan got his first shot as action director with *The Heroine* (also titled *Attack of the Kung Fu Girls*) in which

A seventeen-year-old Chan in *Master with Cracked Fingers* (1971). (*Colin Geddes/Asian Eye*)

stuntman and choreographer, but things just weren't going his way. Accepting his measly role as a stuntman, Chan became almost impervious to pain, taking the hardest falls he could endure in hopes of catching the attention of the directors and fight choreographers. A few opportunities would open up, but Chan's outlook on life needed a fresh approach. In 1975 he moved to Australia to stay with his mother at the American embassy for a year. Bored out of his mind, he would spend much of his time practicing on rooftops and finding odd jobs as a cook and dishwasher. Chan prided himself with the thought of really becoming a kung fu master by wearing himself out day after day.

Chan almost thought of calling it quits, however, until he got a call one day from producer-director Lo Wei. Lo was the man who discovered Bruce Lee and often claimed credit for his success, directing him in *Fists of Fury* and *The Chinese Connection*. Lee's death in 1973 sent a scare into the Hong Kong film community. As Lee was the only Hong Kong star to gain international notoriety, film companies made a valiant effort to find his replacement. It seemed that anyone who could throw a punch or a kick was given a shot, and any variation of Bruce Lee's name was put to good use for marketing. Lo became obsessive in the search and noticed Chan in *Hand of Death* (1975), an early kung fu outing for director John Woo (long before his rise to fame with hits like *The Killer* and America's *Broken Arrow*). (Coincidentally, it was Lo who had directed *The Heroine* for which Chan action-directed.) In viewing the film, it's difficult to see what Lo saw in Chan, since his

he played a bit part. Chan played a bad guy to a female lead in *Police Woman* (1974) with an embarrassingly large patch of hair growing on one cheek! Though the experience was unmemorable, Chan became friends with the lead actor of that film, Chun Cheung-lam. Chan would eventually receive acting lessons from Chun in return for teaching him kung fu.

Chan appeared in a few other films as a

role was nothing more than a bit player to spotlight the talents of Tan Tao-liang, another Bruce Lee imitator and one of the best martial arts actors of the time.

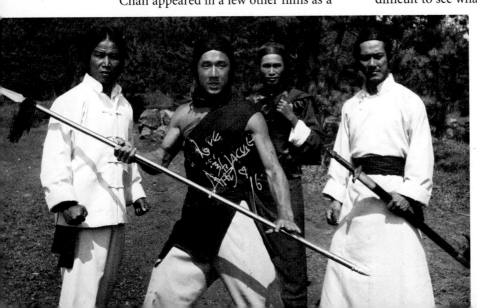

Chan in John Woo's *Hand of Death* (1975). That's Woo behind Chan's left shoulder. (*Colin Geddes/Asian Eye. By permission of Media Asia Group. © STAR TV*)

Lo Wei's films were low-budget, weak affairs held together by ridiculous narratives. Fights are thrown in just to run down the clock for ninety minutes (the length of almost all Hong Kong films for no rhyme or reason). Lo did have an eye for talent, but he couldn't direct or shape that talent. American karate star Chuck Norris was an example: he was wasted as an exploitive villain in *Slaughter in San Francisco,* a film Lo directed for Golden Harvest. As for Jackie Chan, his addition in 1976 to the Lo Wei formula didn't work out as Lo hoped. Lo counted on Chan to carry the movie—something he just couldn't pull off yet. Chan's odd-looking features were matched with low budgets and poor scripting—not a winning formula. Chan didn't have a chance to work on an on-screen persona because Lo was too busy experimenting with varying characterizations within the kung fu genre. Audiences didn't know what to expect from Chan.

Unfortunately for Chan, he would have to prove himself in Lee's mold—something that not only he couldn't do, but no one could ever do. Thinking that he really had found the next Bruce Lee, Lo miscast Chan in *New Fist of Fury* (1976), with Nora Miao and Lo Wei reprising their roles from the Lee film, that actually being *The Chinese Connection*—not *Fist of Fury.* The film picks up where *The Chinese Connection* left off: Miao flees to Taiwan with the Japanese hot on her trail. Once again, the villainous Japanese set out to control all of the martial arts schools, and Miao must find a new leader in the form of Chan, who wants nothing to do with fighting nor caring about anything in general. Motivated by revenge, Chan eventually comes to her aid and leads the way to victory.

Chan's Peking Opera training gave him the ability to perform showy acrobatics, and there

Shaolin Wooden Men (1976). (*Colin Geddes/Asian Eye*)

was no doubt that he was a capable martial artist, but audiences were supposed to be watching the new Bruce Lee, and Chan's less than charismatic portrayal didn't do the film any favors. Chan tried to play the character with the same kind of confidence that Lee brought to the role, but he just wasn't appealing enough to be taken seriously. Chan explains, "Nobody can imitate Bruce Lee. He [Lo] wanted me to do the same kick and the same punch. I think that even now, nobody can do better than Bruce Lee because he is the king of kung fu films in the audience's mind." (Interestingly enough, the only man who has been called the "Best Bruce Lee Imitator" is Sammo Hung, who perfectly copied his mannerisms and fighting style in the 1978 film *Enter the Fat Dragon.*) *New Fist of Fury* was so lackluster compared to its classic predecessor that many wonder whether Bruce Lee had more of a hand in directing the original than Lo. *New Fist of Fury* did mark the first time that Chan adopted his Chinese name of Sing Lung, a nonsensical translation meaning "becoming dragon," or, if not entirely correct, "successful dragon." It was modeled after Bruce Lee's Chinese name of Lee Siu-lung, meaning "little dragon."

Lo produced *Shaolin Wooden Men* the same year, but it didn't make a difference. Using

罗 羅 許 出品人 成王 領衛主演 龍羽 羅 導演
維 維
古
龍 華

蘭毓莉
玉靈龍

薛馬李
漢樓晶鎮
陳陳洞　
源　　　
　王李胡馬薛王　
　雄洞南晃晶河　
環強威場虎中　

雨傘 THE KILLER METEORS

○ WEI MOTION PICTURE CO., LTD. 品出司公限有業影維羅

(Colin Geddes/Asian Eye)

a surprisingly coherent script, Chan plays a worker in a Shaolin temple who has sworn himself to silence until he can avenge his father's death. The only way he can leave the temple is to pass through a series of wooden robots animated as would-be attackers with springs, chains, and pulleys. The devices were actually nothing more than sensationalized versions of the wooden dummies invented by Wing Chun practitioners for training. To run the almost impossible gauntlet, Chan learns various styles of kung fu, making the point that the most successful martial artist is well rounded. Chan emerges victor over the wooden men and goes on to right the wrongs inflicted on his family. Predictable but flashy, the film did create a stir in the community because Chan was able to perform all five styles of animal kung fu as well as use the staff with perfect accuracy. Still, in the end it was just another film.

Unsure of what to make of him, Lo next cast Chan as a bad guy in *The Killer Meteors* (1977), giving yet another hero role for the downward-spiraling career of Jimmy Wang Yu. Wang Yu was second only to Bruce Lee in creating a strong persona with his *One-Arm Swordsman* role. Chan merely laughs into the camera and performs a few flips before attacking the stiff Wang, who had no formal martial arts training. It wasn't much of a role, but Lo thought that Wang Yu's presence would boost Chan's appeal with the audience. He was wrong.

Going downhill even further, Lo directed Chan in the completely absurd *To Kill with Intrigue* (1977), essentially a Chinese melodrama, or "weepie," peppered with kung fu fights. Chan plays a stone-faced survivor of a massacre that left his family dead, and he must contend with the killer, who has fallen in love with him. The only problem is that Chan is bent on finding his pregnant girlfriend, whom he abruptly pushed away at the beginning of the film. As premise-based as the plot already is, it becomes disjointed by more characters, belonging to different martial arts factions, that the audience is supposed to remember. The film brings the love-war relationship to a head when Chan and his female captor work together to battle the real bad guys. A cruel training regimen pits Chan against her in a series of tests. After defeating Chan, she tells him to train and face her again. Chan comes back for more and loses a second time, so she puts a hot coal down his mouth as punishment! With a raspy voice, the determined Chan goes back into training to try and win a third match. His lesson yet unlearned, this time she burns the side of his face off! After figuring that Chan isn't going to

Jackie's Names

Born:	Jacky Chan Kong-sang
Opera name:	Yuen Lau (Yuan Lau)
First film name:	Chan Yuen Lung
Lo Wei name:	Sing Lung (English: Jacky Chan)
Golden Harvest name:	Sing Lung (English: Jackie Chan)
Other names:	Shing Lung, Cheng Long

give up, the lady whirlwind gives Chan a cupful of her own blood, magically transforming him into a kung fu master!

To make matters worse, Lo directs the film like any other pedestrian effort, using low angles to shoot supposed flying sequences, reversing the film for flying backward, and making up weapons, such as a club the size of a man with a face painted on it. Despite these exploitive mechanisms, the film does have some intricate fight choreography that really shows audiences that Chan can fight, perform acrobatics, and leap from tall trees in a single bound. The final fight sequence is undoubtedly the best Chan moment, leaving one to wonder why the rest of the film wasn't as good.

Trying to find some kind of hero within Chan, Lo began grabbing at straws. Chan was paired with Lee's old costar James Tien in several films, and it seemed that the only experimentation his character would undergo was a change in wardrobe and hair styles. Sporting a Shaw Brothers-like ponytail, Chan made his dream project, *Snake and Crane Arts of Shaolin* (1978). Like most kung fu films, the opening credits show off the star's talents, and Chan puts on an incredible show using a spear, broad sword, and tonfa. Chan plays a lone kung fu expert roaming the countryside in possession of a book that contains the secret of the snake and crane arts, naturally. Chan spouts off plentiful wisecracks and must champion numerous entities wishing to get their hands on the book. He eventually teams up with a tomboy, who has her own idea of how the book should be used, and together they must battle their way to the ending, which unfolds the mystery of the book and its deceased writers.

This film contains the best fight choreography before Chan's Seasonal films, and the buddy

Snake and Crane Arts of Shaolin (1977). (Colin Geddes/Asian Eye)

concept works quite well amid the usual Lo(w) Wei production values. Whatever Chan's minor deficiencies in the martial arts department, he was formally trained in the use of classical Chinese weapons (a staple of Cantonese opera) and was able to put these abilities to good use. Despite the energy put into the film, it met with dismal returns at the box office due to a lack of advertising.

With Lo Wei giving the final go-ahead for a comedy, Chan and friend Chen Chi-hwa (*Snake and Crane*'s director) created *Half a Loaf of Kung Fu*. The kung fu film market was so overloaded with every possible variation of kung fu style usage and of plots based on rivaling clans, revenge, and betrayal, that Chan saw the need for a parody. Almost the entire cast from *Snake* was used again, and famed comic character actor Dean Shek was brought in to lighten things up even more. Over the film's opening credits, Chan dresses in various costumes, sets up typical scenes inherent to the kung fu genre, and defuses them with humorous antidotes. In one sequence a bare-chested Chan performs a series of movements, jump-cutting to a shot of a wooden dummy. When Chan comes upon the device, it stands only one foot high, and he kicks and punches at it as though it were full size.

Chan remains deliriously goofy throughout the entire film, while most of the supporting players stay within their conventional molds. Borrowing from Chinese lore that ascribes the power of flight to warriors, kung fu films would often allow its players to leap far into the air, only to land just a few feet away from their intended combatants. When Chan jumps into the air, he flaps his arms like a chicken and squawks at his opponents. Before the film can finally settle down into its serious plotline, a duel has Chan using the villain's hairpiece as nunchakas in typical Bruce Lee fashion. Chan, whose character doesn't know kung fu, is even tricked into learning the "steel finger," a phony technique that doesn't quite work for Chan when put to the test. In one scene, Chan entirely breaks out of character with a laugh as he walks offscreen.

Half a Loaf of Kung Fu is more than worth a look for fans seeking Chan's first real attempts

Chan uses his lovely co-star as a weapon in *Half a Loaf of Kung Fu*—a gimmick he would improve on fourteen years later in *City Hunter*. (*Colin Geddes/Asian Eye*)

at comedy, and despite the in-your-face approach, some of the scenes are quite funny. When Lo saw the film, he quickly shelved it— only to release it in 1980 when Chan's popularity was catching on.

At this point in time, Chan and Lo had nowhere else to turn but to each other. Chan was on a longterm contract, and Lo had no one else in his stable of actors to use as a worthy lead. Lo would probably have had more success if he had stayed with Golden Harvest instead of venturing out on his own, but by 1978, it was too late. The damage had been done, and the two had no other choice but to keep churning out kung fu films.

Trying yet another approach, Lo paired Chan with two other heavies, James Tien and Bruce Lee-alike Bruce Leung, for a group-protagonist kung fu flick entitled *Magnificent Bodyguards*. Boasting some fairly amateurish special effects, the low-budget film was released in 3-D to enliven the shoddy plotline, which has our three heroes escorting a rich family carrying a sick relative to safety. Their journey takes them into harm's way at every turn. They meet up with Chinese natives, monks, and an evil king who controls their safe passage. Midway through the film, Lo's production company stumbled across the score for *Star Wars*, so they pull several tracks for the film's cheapo soundtrack. *Star Wars'* famous trench-battle music even plays over the film's final fight!

Aside from the colorful costumes and corny plot twist at the end, the only two parts of this film worth watching are Leung's excellent kicks and one little piece of dialogue. When the monks can't fight off the trio, they escape behind a series of corridors, and ring a group of large bells overhead to knock out their adversaries. "Well, all of them were pretty tough fighters, but none of them could survive my bells!"

Upset that Chan couldn't make a decent kung fu comedy, Lo decided to direct him in *Spiritual Kung Fu* (1978). While Lo's direction allows for Chan's comic approach to shine, the film tries too hard to be a comedy and fails at almost every turn. Chan plays a lonely temple worker who asks to watch over the library and guard it against oncoming thieves bent on stealing the temple's secrets. When five red-haired female spirits show up, they agree to teach Chan the art of "spiritual kung fu," which gives him the necessary skills to find the thief who stole an important book from the library. Lo's idea of comedy has Chan urinating on an inch-high spirit and cramming small animals down the front of his pants. As the film progresses, the film becomes completely uneven, settling down into the doldrums of typical kung fu fare.

Dragon Fist (1978) is arguably the best of Chan's Lo Wei films, despite the fact that it's a serious kung fu outing. The well-structured script injects depth and emotion into the common revenge story. Although this would have made the perfect Bruce Lee vehicle, audiences get the chance to see Chan act as a straight man. During a martial arts competition, a master from a rival clan comes to challenge the master putting on the competition. The rival not only defeats him but kills him in the process. When one of the students (Chan) returns to find his master killed, he takes the master's wife and daughter along with him to settle the score. But when he finds the rival master, he sees an hon-

Lobby card for *Magnificent Bodyguards* showing Chan's not-so-magnificent hair. (*Colin Geddes/ Asian Eye*)

orable warrior who acknowledges his wrong in killing and has even cut off his own leg in repentance. Chan's honor is tested when another clan forces him to fight the clan that he has forgiven. Chan's fierce bravado, several plot twists, and top-notch fight choreography make *Dragon Fist* a worthy addition to Chan's early filmography.

It didn't matter what film it was—Lo just couldn't make Chan into a star. Chan's Peking Opera training made him more of a dancer, not a seasoned fighter. Still, for Chan, there was a spark of interest in filmmaking: Lo slept through many of the films that he was supposedly directing, giving Chan the chance to direct some scenes himself. By 1978 Lo had just about given up, and when he began to run out of money, he was happy to loan Chan out to Seasonal Films when the opportunity arose. Lo's shortage of money prevented *Spiritual Kung Fu* and *Dragon Fist* from being released at first, but the two would come out in between the two Seasonal films that Chan would make.

The Seasonal Breakthrough

The kung fu film market was growing stagnant. There were many films in release from multiple companies, but Shaw Brothers was the only studio that mattered. Housing all of the greatest martial arts actors and directors, the Shaw Brothers had a virtual monopoly. The Shaw style was built on violent confrontations full of blood and carnage, with directors Chang Cheh and Lau Kar-leung churning films out by the dozen gaining instant notoriety under the Shaw banner.

Ex-Shaw Brothers director-producer Ng See-yuen sought to compete by founding Seasonal Films, and in 1976 he directed the classic *Secret Rivals*. The film set a new precedent in the annals of kung fu cinema by moving away from a "slap hands" emphasis to more acrobatic movements and high kicking. The film's success was partly due to Hwang Jang-lee, generally considered the best kicker in kung fu films. He was a 7th-degree black belt in tae kwon do, which he learned in Korea, the place of the art's origins. Hwang was known for being a rough-and-tumble customer on- and offscreen, and he became one of the most famous kung fu villains outside of the Shaw Brothers' films. As soon as he showed up on screen, audiences didn't have to guess as to what he would be doing.

With several hits and misses, Ng began to see a negative side to this type of action: "I have always marketed my kung fu films all over the world, but certain countries, such as Scandinavia, would ban those films because of the

Chan disapproves of Sam Seed's (Simon Yuen Siu-tin) teaching methods in the Seasonal hit *Drunken Master.* **(Colin Geddes/Asian Eye)**

SNAKE IN THE EAGLE'S SHADOW

Snake in the Eagle's Shadow (1978). (*Courtesy of Seasonal Films*)

violence. Indeed, kung fu films didn't have to be so violent, so I wanted to try throwing in some comedy." Ironically, Chan was brought to Ng by Yuen Woo-ping, who was one of Ng's top fight choreographers. When Chan was thinking of giving up on his career after the unsuccessful *Snake and Crane Arts of Shaolin*, he met Yuen Woo-ping, who gave him the hope and inspiration to continue in the business. Chan had already worked with Yuen's brother, Yuen Cheung-yan (who served as the film's choreog-

Simon Yuen Siu-tin, veteran Shaw Brothers actor and father of the director of *Snake in the Eagle's Shadow*. (*Courtesy of Seasonal Films*)

rapher), on the 1973 film *Eagle Shadow Fist* (not the original title of the film but merely a later attempt to cash-in on Ng's later, successful *Snake in the Eagle's Shadow*). Cheap and bloody, the film has Chan playing the brother of the star, who must fight off the Japanese during the Sino-Japanese War that started in 1937. The only aspect of the film worth a look is the opening, which shows Chan in Peking Opera garb with full makeup.

Chan was originally teamed up with Ng for *Tower of Death*, a sequel to *Game of Death* using a Lee look-alike with leftover footage from *Enter the Dragon*. *Tower of Death* would take three years to complete, but luckily, Chan didn't end up in the film. He was ready for something else.

That something else was *Snake in the Eagle's Shadow*. The director would be Yuen Woo-ping, who, coincidentally, had also been a student of Master Yu at the Chinese Opera Research Institute. Yuen had been with Ng since 1971, and he and his four brothers were starting to work together as group choreographers. Actually, it was Yuen who secured Chan his lead role in *Snake*. Ng was looking at young kung fu star Cliff Lok, who happened (ironically) to look like Chan—with even a similar nose. Yuen wanted Chan because they knew each other and because they were both proponents of the northern style of kung fu. Despite worries from distributors that Chan wasn't marketable, Ng went with Yuen's choice. Yuen Woo-ping's father, Simon Yuen Siu-tin, was a veteran Shaw Brothers actor and had been an instructor at the Chinese Opera Research Institute. At sixty-seven years of age, Yuen Siu-tin could still fight and perform acrobatics, and he made a logical choice for playing Chan's mentor in the film. With a firm understanding of Peking Opera, Yuen Woo-ping quickly assessed the most efficient way to use Chan in a film. His brothers also put their varied knowledge of choreography

THE SEASONAL BREAKTHROUGH

to good use, with brother Brandy Yuen Chun-yeung as fight director.

Adding balance to Chan's playful acrobatic skill, Hwang Jang-lee was hired to put his sure-footed knowledge of direct fighting to good use. Ng had problems at first in clearing Hwang's visa for Hong Kong, but he persisted, and Hwang was set to play the only conventional kung fu characterization in the film. Hwang and Chan reportedly did not get along on the set—especially since Hwang accidentally kicked Chan's front tooth out during a fight scene. Toward the end of the film, one can clearly see the gap in Chan's teeth as he ferociously battles Hwang.

At a time when structured kung fu scripts were a rarity, *Snake in the Eagle's Shadow* brought a humorous framework into the otherwise violent world of the genre with perfect timing. The film clearly defines the kung fu comedy, in the process breaking all box office records in Hong Kong, making Chan a star, and undoubtedly creating the "Seasonal formula."

Shaw Brothers films made good candidates to lampoon. Chan's character was a country bumpkin who had no knowledge of martial arts, which was perhaps lifted from the Shaw Brothers film *Spiritual Boxer* (1975), directed by Lau Kar-leung. Chan plays an orphan working for a local kung fu school whose teachers (one of whom is played by Dean Shek) have mastered the art of ripping off their students, using Chan as their punching bag. Yuen Siu-tin, as the last of the snake-fist fighters, is a tired, old vagabond who has run out of steam in fleeing from Hwang and his henchmen (all of whom are proponents of the Eagle Claw style). The film brings Yuen and Chan together to form a unique bond, not unlike father and son. In gratitude for being given shelter and food, Yuen inscribes on the wall a series of movements to help the young Chan learn martial arts.

Hwang Jang-lee takes his fighting scenes a little *too* seriously—taking out one of Chan's front teeth in the process. (*Courtesy of Seasonal Films*)

Chan has difficulty visualizing the motion, but when he steps outside, he finds the movements traced on the ground before him like orchestrated dance steps. This scene signifies Chan's rebirth in the cinema as a physical entertainer not hampered by traditional ways or realism. As respected Hong Kong film critic Roger Garcia explains, "Consciousness reveals itself by describing a process, shuttling to and fro, from text to movement, from movement to text, to check their accuracy and effect; to produce a mobile writing, a text in activation."

When Chan loses his dignity at the hands of his teachers and runs sobbing into seclusion, he meets up with Yuen once again, only to find he has been injured at the hands of Hwang's men. This scene reinforces Chan's good-naturedness, as he is willing to care for the needs of others even when facing adversity himself. The two then begin training together, straying far from anything that can be called traditional. These montages would make anything from *Rocky* look easy, as Chan's body twists and turns about, stretching the limits of plausibility if it weren't for the wide angle shots that prove he's doing everything himself. Athleticism has always been a requirement for kung fu stars, but

(*Courtesy of Seasonal Films*)

Chan takes his physical abilities further than most.

"Hong Kong was going through a very troubled time, and the kids really could identify with the rebellion aspect of Chan's character," says former Hong Kong film critic Shu Kei. "The other kung fu films were based on structured, stiff movements, while *Snake in the Eagle's Shadow* was loose." From the opening credits, where Chan performs a freestyle kata, to the finale, *Snake in the Eagle's Shadow* wasn't lambasting kung fu films but merely having fun with the traditional values, trading them in for a liberated sense of movement. For starters, the

film opts for a disco-synthesized theme song that spotlights Chan's youthful, unsupervised character. His acrobatic, almost Olympiclike movements run perfectly to the beat. Some of the dramatic melodies sound like the *Star Trek* theme, and even a Spanish tune is used for good effect. All of the music sounds familiar, and even if it is lifted from another source, its use in a kung fu film works just fine.

Even venturing out in more dangerous territory is a poke at the West. In many Chinese films, missionaries and other Western characters are seen proselytizing Chinese wanderers. One such character in *Snake*, who even resembles Jesus, roams the streets calling out to those who don't know God. When he comes into contact with Yuen, he is revealed to be one of Hwang's men in disguise, turning his shiny cross into a dagger. He then lashes out at Yuen with a flurry of kicks and punches; he tussles with Chan later in the film. The character was played by Roy Horan, cofounder of Seasonal Films.

The final call for uprooting the traditionalism of kung fu films comes from kung fu itself. Chan discovers his newfound snake-fist style can't defeat Hwang's eagle claw, so he must find a different way. While kung fu has a battery of forms based on animals, Chan finds his inspira-

Hwang Jang-lee and Chan's classic fight in *Snake in the Eagle's Shadow*. (*Courtesy of Seasonal Films*)

tion in an ordinary house cat which he sees fighting off a cobra. Although an animal protection agency would have sued the company for its treatment of animals (one can see a rope tying the cat to a live cobra!), Chan combines his observation of motion with the snake-fist for a deadly combination. In a hilarious climatic sequence set on a beach, Chan jumps around hissing like a cat, leaping into the air, arching his back, and crinkling his hands into claws to defeat Hwang.

Chan remembers all too well the reaction in an interview for *Hong Kong Film Connection*. "The audience was surprised: 'Where the hell did this boy come from?' At that time, for almost twenty years I had been fighting, and nobody goes to the theater to see me, but suddenly it's the right time. I kid around—totally opposite to Bruce Lee. When Bruce Lee kick high, I kick low. When Bruce Lee acts like a hero, I act like an underdog. Nobody can beat Bruce Lee; everybody can beat me. He's not smiling; I'm always smiling. This is why *Snake in the Eagle's Shadow* totally changes the action film."

Instead of playing off of a script that stumbles with comic material, *Snake in the Eagle's Shadow* presented a new kind of slapstick comedy. While a slapstick act like the Three Stooges used assorted gags and sound effects to pull off their crude physical abuses, the film's intricate choreography brought charm and grace to the comic form. The comedy was not accented by overacting or cheap props, it had a genuine place in the film, and it worked well with the light melodrama of Chan's and Yuen's underdog characters.

With the success of *Snake*, Seasonal didn't have to think hard to come up with its follow-up film, *Drunk Monkey in the Tiger's Eye*, known internationally as *Drunken Master*. Instead of

Dean Shek tries to break Chan's horse stance in *Drunken Master* (1978). (*Colin Geddes/Asian Eye*)

playing just another bumpkin character, Chan plays the Chinese folklore legend Hwang Fei-hung, a real-life hero who has been exaggerated in Chinese cinema to the point of comparing him to Robin Hood in America. Although the character has been portrayed over 100 times on-screen since the first Hong Kong films were made in the late twenties and early thirties, Chan's take was quite different than the valiant, honorable Chinese hero. In fact, he shows no signs of anything that the real or cinematic Hwang would do except for having a good heart. As with *Snake*, it's all about breaking down the genre's traditionalism.

In the beginning of the film, Hwang's father punishes him by forcing the lad to take the horse stance position for hours on end, placing cups of tea on his hands to add pain to punishment. The horse stance is the very foundation of Hung Gar, the martial arts system that the real Hwang Fei-hung practiced. In finding the

DRUNK MONKEY IN
THE TIGER'S EYE

Clockwise, from upper left: Hwang Jang-lee
teaches Chan a lesson about drying his
clothes. (*Colin Geddes/Asian Eye*)
Chan puts Yuen's teaching to good use in the
climactic fight of *Drunken Master*. (*Colin
Geddes/Asian Eye*)
Once more, Simon Yuen puts Chan through a
series of unorthodox training procedures.
(*Colin Geddes/Asian Eye*)

help the elderly, and even going toe to
toe with his aunt when he mistakenly
belittles his own niece! Tired of dealing with him, his father puts him
under the supervision of Sam the
Seed (played by Simon Yuen), a
drunken beggar known for his fierce
training rituals. When Chan flees his
new "master" because he doesn't care
about discipline, he runs into an assassin
(Hwang Jang-lee), who has actually been sent to
kill Chan's father for something he did.

experience unbearable, Hwang cheats by using a
small chair for support. This sequence was also
inspired by Chan's Peking Opera days, where
Master Yu would make the students stand
motionless to teach them control. The tea cups
were added to see which students could make it
through the torture without breaking.

Chan's Hwang gets into trouble at every
turn by picking fights with the locals, trying to

When the assassin disgraces Chan in every
way, Chan once again runs back to Yuen to
learn the art of drunken-boxing. Drunken-
boxing, a real form of kung fu, mimics the
swaying of a drunkard, but the film actually
requires the character to get inebriated in order

to fight. Chan's scenes of doing just that are absolutely hysterical, and he must learn the eight drunken-boxing styles to contend with Hwang Jang-lee in the fifteen-minute finale. Chan goes through each of seven styles, only to find himself one short because he didn't think the last style would be effective. As Yuen coaches from the sidelines, the eighth style forces Chan to fight like a girl, with a high-pitched voice and ladylike gestures.

Drunken Master's ending scene is clearly influenced by the climax of *Spiritual Boxer*, and the drunken vagabond can be traced to another Shaw Brothers classic, *Heroes of the East* (1978). The choreography is even more intricate than that of *Snake in the Eagle's Shadow*, and Chan's wisecracking would permanently become part of his on-screen persona (not unlike his own). While *Snake* creates a relationship between rebellion (Chan) and tradition (Yuen), the bond doesn't quite mesh together as well as in *Drunken Master*, where the two men actually have to share quarters and learn to understand each other. Chan's character has to learn the tradition set forth by his father.

Drunken Master outgrossed any of Bruce Lee's films, and it was the second highest grossing film for the year in Hong Kong. Although Raymond Chow has often been credited for breaking Chan into Japan, it was actually Ng See-yuen, whose persistence and courage cracked this new market. Ng recalls, "It was very difficult to promote Jackie in Japan because no one knew who he was, and magazines even refused to run his picture." Finally, Toei agreed to distribute the film in 1982 under the title *Drunk Monkey*. *Snake* would soon follow, ensuring Chan's success in Japan. *Drunken Master* also broke box office records in Singapore and Malaysia and was well received in American theaters, the drunken device giving it an extra kick.

Famed critic and Hong Kong film expert Ric Meyers remembers catching the film in 1980 at a New York Chinatown theater: "Seeing these people move the way they were moving and doing what they were doing was sheer amazement. It was almost as if the shackles had been removed from the cinema. It was like Steve

Reeves breaking the chains in *Hercules Unchained*. It had that kind of release and exhilaration . . . an eruption of thrills. There was *somebody*, somewhere, who knew how to do it—and did it unapologetically without slicing it up or talking down to the audience." While it's clear that Ng See-yuen and Yuen Woo-ping were much more than minor contributors to the film's success, the audience acclaimed that somebody to be Jackie Chan.

With the success of both Seasonal films, Chan returned to a more supportive Lo Wei, who let him direct his first film, *The Fearless Hyena*, for his wife's company, Goodyear Films. While the structure is clearly lifted from what made the Seasonal films a success, Chan incorporates more comedy and invention despite the lower production values. In following the Seasonal formula, Chan came up with "emotional kung fu," yet another device to add novelty to the master-student training montage. This time out Chan plays a wisecracking youth who finds a job as a fighter for a bogus school,

Chan continues the Seasonal formula in his directorial debut, *The Fearless Hyena*. (Colin Geddes/Asian Eye)

Chan plays on Yen Shi-kwan's emotions. (*Colin Geddes/Asian Eye*)

catures is important for the sake of diversity. American actor-comedian Robin Williams is a prime example, since he can execute any kind of accented character to perfection on screen—most notably with the genie in *Aladdin*. Even though Chan is stuck in the period kung fu realm, he is able to create three distinct personalities to show his versatility. Because his grandfather fears the attention his sacred technique, Hsing Yi, would attract, he requests that Chan not be seen or heard fighting. So Chan disguises himself: His first personality is a gritty voiced, cross-eyed bum who fights with a small bench against his opponent. In mixing it up with a bulky giant, Chan faces his second combatant dressed as a girl, adding

but he catches the attention of a rival kung fu master when he starts showing off the techniques his grandfather (James Tien) had taught him. When the master follows Chan back to his home and kills his grandfather, Chan immediately sets out for revenge but is stopped by one of his grandfather's old friends. Chan is taught emotional kung fu: to play upon his enemy's emotions through his own happiness, laughter, sadness, and anger. And like in *Drunken Master*, he has to use all these emotions to reach victory. The sadness emotion is particularly comical, as Chan runs at his opponent crying while acrobatically dodging his blows. The villain is played by Yen Shi-kwan (the handicapped master from *Dragon Fist*), who would later play a series of similar roles, starting with the film that in 1991 formally brought period piece kung fu films back to Hong Kong cinema, *Once Upon a Time in China*.

Many have dismissed *The Fearless Hyena* for its obvious rip-off qualities, but Chan does bring his comic persona to new levels. While every comedian has a certain style that he or she adheres to, the ability to compose alternate cari-

French poster for *The Fearless Hyena*. (*Colin Geddes/Asian Eye*)

Un film écrit, interprété et réalisé par

JACKIE CHAN

La Hyène Intrépide

Yuen Shun-yee takes over for Jackie in *Dance of the Drunk Mantis* in 1979. (*Colin Geddes/Asian Eye*)

After Chan's Seasonal films and *Fearless Hyena*, everyone was trying to cash in on the formula. Yuen Woo-ping directed brother Yuen Shun-yee, replacing Chan, in *Dance of the Drunk Mantis*, which was billed as the sequel to *Drunken Master*. Yuen Woo-ping would become the greatest director of period piece kung fu films, and he is still churning them out with great speed and invention even today. Because of the Seasonal films, Yuen Siu-tin became a big star once again, and everyone wanted him to play the eccentric, old beggar in films like *Story of the Drunken Master*, *World of the Drunken Master*, and *Sleeping Fist*. He was even used with another *Snake* and *Drunken Master* veteran, Dean Shek, to complete *Master of Cracked Fingers* with a Chan look-alike. Even Hwang Jang-lee tried his hand at the Seasonal formula with *Hitman in the Hand of Buddha* (1980), which he directed, produced, and starred in. Hwang would enjoy a long career, with more than forty film credits, before settling down in his homeland of Korea, where he owns a golf tee factory and hotel. Ng See-yeun would give Yuen Kwai, one of Chan's Peking Opera brothers, a shot at directing with *Ninja in a Dragon's Den* (1982), featuring Conan Lee, another Chan rip-off artist. Ng would later discover Jean-Claude Van Damme, producing him in *No Retreat, No Surrender* (1985). The best cash-in film, starring Indonesian martial artist Billy Chong, was *Crystal Fist* (1979). Choreographed by Yuen Woo-ping and his brothers and costarring Yuen Siu-tin, it stood on its own. In fact, *Crystal Fist* is better in many ways than Chan's two Seasonal films. Chong had boyish good looks, and his martial arts and acrobatic abilities easily matched, if not exceeded, Chan's. Chong had the potential to be a major screen hero, but, sadly, only made a handful of films before dropping out of sight. Audiences were bombarded with these Seasonal cash-in films since they could be churned out in weeks.

further to the feminine actions he performed at the end of *Drunken Master*. Punctuating his vagabond costume with a pencil-thin mustache, Chan next fights a sword-wielding player, with a series of belittling comments to add pain to punishment.

The film's best moment is a fight with three spearmen, much like the one from the previous year's *Snake and Crane Arts of Shaolin* (even using two of that film's actors, who played similar roles). The problem with much of Chan's earlier choreography was the absence of rhythm. Much of the motion on the screen would start and stop with each individual movement, hinting at the fact that the action was choreographed like numbered dance steps. The spear scene in *The Fearless Hyena* is especially intricate, but it's

filmed with perfect fluidity, enhancing the flowing energy. It is the best single choreographed moment in Chan's seventies résumé.

Lo Wei may have failed in picking films for him, but the Lo Wei tenure did benefit Chan in some ways. Aside from giving Chan the stage name (Sing Lung) he still goes by, Lo concentrated on making Chan look better. He fixed his teeth and paid for an operation to cut his eyelids, a normal process for many Chinese actors. It's generally known that "wide-eyed" stars are more appealing and successful internationally.

One of Lo's production assistants, Willie Chan Chi-keung (no relation), not only became good friends with Chan but saw a diamond in the rough. He knew that Chan's only hope for success was to leave Lo Wei. Hong Kong has dif-

Chan sets up a publicity shot for *Island of Fire*, his "debt."
(Colin Geddes/Asian Eye)

ferent ethics—unlike Hollywood's cutthroat practices. Ng See-yuen felt that he would have broken a code of honor in trying to steal Chan away from Lo. "Golden Harvest was talking to Jackie, and they were trying everything they could to get him," says Ng. In the end Ng stayed away, and together Jackie Chan and Willie Chan made the move to Golden Harvest. Founded by ex-Shaw employee Raymond Chow Man-wai, Golden Harvest was the second largest Hong Kong film company next to the Shaw Brothers studio. Jackie & Willie Productions was soon formed to concentrate on Chan's personal power outside of Golden Harvest. While the actors who worked with Chan during the Lo Wei period faded away, Chan's friendship with director Chen Chi-hwa prospered. He would go on to serve as second unit director on many of Chan's blockbuster efforts, among them *Police Story*, both *Project A*'s, and *Mr. Canton and Lady Rose*.

In an ambitious attempt, Lo Wei cut together unused scenes from *Fearless Hyena* and *Spiritual Kung Fu* to create *Fearless Hyena II*. Chan tried to sue Lo, who wanted to release it in 1983, but the film came out anyway. Lo would eventually drift off into obscurity, having lost both Bruce Lee and Jackie Chan to Golden Harvest. His films never had a polished look, and even if they did, they didn't have Bruce Lee or Jackie Chan anymore to keep the audience interested. In 1993 Lo tried once more to make a successful, traditional kung fu film by hiring Sammo Hung to direct the lavish *Blade of Fury*. The film did have some strong points, but audiences just weren't interested. Lo would die three years later at the age of 77 with over 65 directing credits to his name.

There have been many rumors and myths surrounding Chan's move to Golden Harvest. Of course, Lo Wei fought Golden Harvest over Chan's contract. Lo was upset with Golden Harvest for pushing him aside after he directed Bruce Lee's first two films—and then they wanted Chan. To facilitate the transition, Golden Harvest brought in Jimmy Wang Yu to negotiate on their behalf. What happened next remains a mystery. One story has it that Wang was held hostage inside a restaurant in Tsimshatsui. Another claims that Wang intervened and stopped a contract put on Chan's life by an angry Lo. Whichever is the true story, Golden Harvest did succeed in attaining Chan, paying his yearly salary to Lo and agreeing to let Lo keep the rights to Chan's old films. Wang was rewarded for his assistance: Chan's cooperation in two Wang films—this would be the "debt" Chan owed him.

Two ominous collaborations, then, would work themselves into Chan's filmography. The first film, *Fantasy Mission Force* (1980), used Chan in a small role, but that didn't stop Wang from publicizing him as the lead. Chan couldn't have worked on the film for more than a few days since much of his "appearance" is achieved with doubles in his place. The film was a contrived, ridiculous mess. Only a scene where Chan fights off a bunch of Amazons is of any interest. Chan would later help Wang again in *Island of Fire* (1991), another low-budget misfire that Chan regrets starring in. Chan noted that the film had a lot of talent but the director, Chu Yen-ping, would just let everyone clown around on the set. The resulting work never settles on one main plotline but rather gives each star his

own personal story. In the finale, Chan and Sammo Hung go on a suicide mission. Infuriated by the project, Chan bought the film and shelved it, so it could not be released in theaters in Hong Kong. Unfortunately, it made it to videotape not only in Hong Kong but everywhere else. Aside from Chan's fancy pool shooting and basic fight action, which he did not choreograph, *Island of Fire* (also known as *Island on Fire*) is a waste of talent.

THREE

A Golden Harvest

Chan had actually started much of his film career with Golden Harvest. With Sammo Hung's help, Chan secured small roles not only in the Bruce Lee films but *Hand of Death* and several of the Huang Feng efforts that Hung was action directing. In 1973 Chan starred as a Japanese villain in *The Heroine*. In another early Golden Harvest effort, *All in the Family* (1975), Chan is seen embarrassingly groping a topless girl in bed.

With the market changing so rapidly in the late seventies, Raymond Chow was banking on Jackie Chan. After Bruce Lee, Chow's only claim to fame had been launching Angela Mao as the female version of Lee, and her high-kicking abilities made her an instant success internationally. Like Ng See-yuen, Chow knew how the system worked and knew that Chan would make a worthy replacement for Bruce Lee in terms of box office—even if Chan's style was different. With more control and money to work with, it was necessary for Chan to put the coup de grace on his kung fu days with *Young Master* (1980), his first film with Golden Harvest as a full-fledged star.

In the wake of all the Seasonal cash-in films that kept chipping away at traditional values, Chan returned to those values, but he had an agenda. He wanted to bring his own choreography talents to classical kung fu sequences, but it was also important to have a story promoting moral values like loyalty, trust, and brotherhood. Chan wanted to stay away from the revenge plots that drove most kung fu films. Lo Wei had released two of his earlier films in the

Korean hapkido master Whang Inn-sik tries to dispose of Jackie Chan in the finale of *Dragon Lord*. (*Colin Geddes/Asian Eye. By permission of Media Asia Group. © STAR TV*)

Young Master (1980). (*Colin Geddes/Asian Eye. By permission of Media Asia Group. © STAR TV*)

must come to his aid by defeating the enemy. The only problem is, Chan is mistaken for Tiger, and the Sheriff and his men go after him.

Like his character, who alone saves the day, Jackie Chan is the only one who can make the film work, since he doesn't want the script or his costars to share the spotlight. All of the kung fu sequences are brilliantly choreographed and boast Chan's limitless physical abilities. From the opening lion dance, which contains an amazing one-shot wonder—the rear end of the lion kicks the cabbage into Chan's hands in the front—*Young Master* is full of invention. When Chan goes to the rival school to find Tiger, he must then prove himself against an obese worker, Chan wielding a fan in defense. In another great one-shot, Chan kicks the open fan straight up into the air and catches it with the greatest of ease. It took Chan over five hundred takes to get that shot just right! Chan also tosses around a broadsword, fighting off the Sheriff's men, and even goes up against his Peking Opera brother Yuen Biao with a sawhorse, or small bench. As a final tip of his hat to the Seasonal formula, he must fight off a girl, who whips him using the skirt style of kung fu, where all of the leg movements are hidden by a large skirt. He would later bring this style into his own repertoire when he has to fight the master's two henchmen.

The final fight, however, has garnered the film more praise than any other scene. Chan must fight off Whang Inn-sik, a master of another Korean martial art known as hapkido. Whang started his career in 1972 when his students, Sammo Hung and Angela Mao, urged him to play the villain in *Hapkido,* which also starred his master, Choi Joy-san, the art's founder. Chan worked on this film as a stunt-man and noticed him in several of the other

midst of Chan's Seasonal success, so Chan's popularity was still questionable. Many critics believed that if *Young Master* didn't make money, Chan's career would be over.

In *Young Master* Chan once again plays a student in a kung fu school whose mission is to win a lion dance competition against a rival school. Lion dance competitions serve as a way for schools to show their expertise, and in film they were constantly used as a device to set up rival schools against one another. These are by no means friendly competitions—winning is everything. When the school's best student, Tiger, is injured and cannot participate, Chan is picked as his replacement. Chan discovers that Tiger has betrayed the school by operating the rival's lion. Chan loses to his former "brother," but he keeps Tiger's betrayal a secret. Tiger eventually leaves the school entirely for monetary gain.

Chan sets off to find his former schoolmate and bring him back to his senses. Tiger instead returns to the rival school, which uses him to rescue its imprisoned master from the local police. The master's lackeys set up Tiger to take the blame for a robbery that follows, and Chan

Huang Feng-directed outings of the early seventies. Whang also played the Japanese fighter who gave Bruce Lee a run for his money in *Return of the Dragon.* Coincidentally, *Young Master* features two other Lee veterans: Tien Fong played the good school's headmaster, as well as a similar role in *The Chinese Connection,* and the sheriff, Shek Kin, played the infamous Dr. Han in *Enter the Dragon.* When Golden Harvest gave way to using Korean fighting systems in kung fu films, tae kwon do was the dominant form.

Chan wanted more for the end fight of *Young Master.* He brought in the complete system of hapkido, which not only uses the lighting-fast kicks and punches, but throws and joint locks as well for variety. In a thrilling twenty-minute duel, Chan is pummeled at every turn, whining and wincing over his inability to match Whang's skills. Between his exhausting bouts with Whang, Chan finds a coach in the form of the rival school's servant, who gives Chan advice, water, and a little extra breathing room.

Chan fights off the Sheriff's men in *Young Master.* . .
. . . then is whipped by the Sheriff's daughter. (*Colin Geddes/Asian Eye. By permission of Media Asia Group. © STAR TV*)

After being kicked to the ground in what looks like a final blow, Chan immediately stands back up, forcing a puzzled look from his foe. The only way for Chan's body to have endured such a hit is plain numbness. "I remember Chan thinking of a way to come back and win in that scene," Whang says, "and all of the sudden, he ran across a viewing of the 'Incredible Hulk.'" Finding inspiration in the Marvel Comics mean green hero, Chan becomes a raging madman, running at Whang and using no structure or direct force but sheer, raw energy as his combative form.

Chan may have saved the day, but he ended the film completely covered in bandages. Before the credits could roll, the bandaged Chan looks straight into the camera and waves bye-bye, signifying his retirement from the kung fu genre. When he broke down into a whirlwind of ener-

gy at the end of the film, cashing in his disciplined technique, he was leaving anything that could be considered kung fu in the dust. Chan was ready to move on to a more complicated form of cinema, with a broader range of storylines and action set pieces.

Young Master did, however, set many precedents for the beginning of Chan's personalized film legacy. The fight scenes were some of the most intricately choreographed sequences he had done. Every scene showed Chan's physical prowess. With the finale making *Young Master* a classic, it broke all box office records in Hong Kong, and it defined Chan's new market in Japan. This was also the first time that Chan had released a film during the Chinese New Year,

Chan puts his gymnastic skills to the test against Whang's two henchmen, Lee Hoi-san (*left*) and Fong Hak-on (*right*). (*Colin Geddes/Asian Eye. By permission of Media Asia Group. © STAR TV*)

whose date ranges from the end of January to early March. From then on he would use Chinese New Year as the date for everyone around Asia to know that a new Jackie Chan film would be released.

Chan began assembling his own crew with *Young Master*, as well. He wanted to create his own team of young, energetic players whom he could plug into any of his films in various roles. Fighting, stunt work, and acting were requirements.

Fong Hak-on was the first person that Chan brought onto his personal team. Fong, a veteran of many Shaw Brothers films, has always played a villain. He can be seen over the opening credits of *Snake in the Eagle's Shadow* and Chan's first fight in *Drunken Master*. Fong and Chan collaborated as fight choreographers on the project *The 36 Crazy Fist* (1979), as a favor to Chan's longtime director pal Chen Chi-wah. Fans can see a fifteen-minute documentary of Chan and Fong choreographing *The 36 Crazy Fist* tacked on to the video of a poorly produced kung fu flick entitled *The Young Tiger*. (In several shots Chan has a cigarette hanging out of his mouth.) *Young Master*'s fight choreography credits listed only Chan and Fong, since this was before Chan devised an entire stuntman team. Also, Fong plays one of Master Whang's two lackeys in the film, and he went on to play the lead fighter in *Police Story* (1986). Fong is in the background of most of Chan's films, but after *Mr. Canton and Lady Rose*, he left Chan's team to pursue his own career as an action director.

Another Shaw Brothers actor, Cheung Ka-nin, was the other early cornerstone of Chan's team. Assuming the stage name Tai Po, meaning "bad boy," his characters would always be mischievous whether he was one of Chan's partners in crime or not. Although Tai Po had martial arts training, Chan wasn't necessarily using him as just another fighter; he was one of Chan's first recurring background players. In *Young Master* Tai plays one of Chan's fellow students in the school.

Young Master was the first film to contain a track sung by Chan. Interestingly enough, the song never made it into the Chinese version, but when the film was released internationally, "Kung Fu Fighting Man" can be heard over the

end credits. Chan's English was almost nonsensical at this point in time, but one can make out
most of the silly lyrics. This would become a
trademark for Chan: All of his later directorial
efforts contain a new ode to heroism sung by
Chan during the credits. They would all be in
Chinese.

With the success of *Young Master*, Chan
was ready for something modern, and that
meant going to America. Bruce Lee's success had
given Golden Harvest a future in the international market, and Raymond Chow was just
itching to try again with Chan. In a calculated
move, he met with his *Enter the Dragon* cohorts,
Fred Weintraub and Robert Clouse, who came
up with the project *Battlecreek Brawl*, later retitled for Western audiences as *The Big Brawl*.
Chan was paid one million dollars for his role,
as he began a two-year tour of duty in America.

Critics often find Chan's first American
effort lackluster, but he learned a few things—
especially the English language. While Bruce Lee
was formally educated in America and had no
problem with English, Chan was just the opposite. He spent two years in Los Angeles studying
with a Beverly Hills language coach seven hours
a day. His secondary training was watching television—he has often credited commercials for

Chan makes the best of a Hollywood fight scene. (*Colin
Geddes/Asian Eye. By permission of Media Asia Group.
© STAR TV*)

teaching him simple American phrases and
ideals.

Chan's first bout with America does show
his charisma and physical abilities, but *The Big
Brawl* sets up limitations on both. A third limitation was a structured script. While Robert

Chan and Mako in a lobby card for *The Big Brawl* (1980). (*By permission of Media Asia Group. © STAR TV*)

Ric Meyers remembers "talking with Jackie after *The Big Brawl*, and he told the famous story about how Robert Clouse told him to go from the door of the car to the door of the restaurant. 'Okay, I jump out, somersault, cartwheel, then I flip around.' 'No, Jackie, no, no, no,' the director said. Finally, Jackie says, 'Nobody pays money to see Jackie walk.' "

whose only ambitions are to marry his girlfriend and compete in roller skating races. He is put to the test when his father is forced to pay protection money to some local mobsters in order to operate a restaurant. Although he is forbidden to fight, Chan comes to his father's aid by fighting off three of the mobsters in and around a car. The entire scene was filmed with a master shot giving only one view of the action. This is a great limitation on Chan's abilities since he has little room to work with, and most Hollywood action directors do little else except move the camera. Segment shooting—where a prescribed set of movements

Clouse's treatment uses some of Chan's underlying qualities, such as playing an underdog, it proves that most of what makes Chan so amazing is his on-the-spot invention. When Bruce Lee, Weintraub, and Clouse collaborated on *Enter the Dragon*, Lee was a part of the team, coming up with many ideas on the set and choreographing all of the fight scenes. For *The Big Brawl*, Chan was just an actor. Unlike Lee, he had no experience with Hollywood's ways, and he wasn't afforded the chance. "I knew that racism was alive and well and living in Hollywood in a very aggressive way," points out Ric Meyers. "I knew that they were treating him like this little Chinese curiosity instead of the true giant that he was. They were treating him like a little man that they were doing a favor for."

Whether he liked it or not, Chan was America's new Bruce Lee, and veteran fight choreographer Pat Johnson was supposed to ensure that. *The Big Brawl's* opening credit sequence has Chan leaping into the air in slow motion, screaming with a long yelp as he throws a few kicks and punches. The movie is set in Chicago during the 1930s, with Chan playing a cocky do-gooder

German ad slick for *The Big Brawl*. (*Colin Geddes/Asian Eye*)

Jackie Chan's Real-Life Brawls

Even today, when someone says "kung fu," the first thought that comes to mind is Bruce Lee. On- and off-screen, Lee wasn't plagued by Chinese stereotypes. He wasn't a docile, subservient being. He was a man in control of his destiny. He was in command of everything he did and had no problem fighting to get there. On numerous occasions Lee was put to the test: first, for teaching the *gwailo* (slang term literally meaning "white ghost," used to describe non-Asians) kung fu; second, for proudly walking the earth—almost imposing the fact that he was a grand example of what a martial artist can be. And challenged he was, but each time Lee would prove to be the victor.

This was Lee's way, not Chan's. In 1980, when Chan was brought into the public eye as the new "master," it was only a matter of time before he, too, would be tested. Arriving in Detroit, Michigan, Chan's first such encounter would take place in the front of city hall, whose front door was hung with a banner reading "Jackie Chan—Master of Kung Fu." The crowd became animated over this proclamation, and Chan felt uneasy. While Chan was in the midst of a kung fu routine, a man jumped up onstage and yelled to Chan a question concerning an attack. The event's promoters stood silently. The man suddenly threw a punch toward Chan, but a well-placed kick to his legs by Chan's left foot sent him to the ground before he could get even close.

That fight was over, but Cincinnati, Ohio, brought on yet another. On a local television show, Chan was to demonstrate a maneuver to escape a choke hold from behind. Unlike in rehearsal, Chan's six-foot partner squeezed as hard as he could, nearly suffocating Chan in the process. With a quick elbow jab to the ribs, Chan spun his body around while sending his opponent to the ground before him.

Finally, in Portland, Oregon, a man walked right up to Chan and challenged him to a fight. After Chan declined, the man held out his hand for a friendly shake. Feeling his hand grasped forcefully, though, Chan readied himself in a defensive position and simply increased the pressure of his own grip. Noticing a quick movement of the man's left hand, Chan grabbed his thumb and bent it to his wrist, sending him to the ground.

When Chan came to America again in 1995, no one dared make such a challenge. With his bodyguard, Kenneth Low Houi-kang, and usually a policeman, Chan could just smile for the cameras and be charming without looking behind his back.

are encompassed in one shot—best displays the dynamism of Chan's action. With only a master shot to move in, Chan had to work his magic one-dimensionally.

Chan's brief encounter catches the eye of the mob boss, who is looking for a new fighter to bet on in an "everything goes" competition called the Battle Creek Brawl in Texas. Chan is forced to participate in the event after being trained under the watchful eye of his uncle, played by Asian character actor Mako. The linear script contains few surprises, and with all of the action scenes filmed with master shots, audiences can see that Chan can do something— they just don't really know what it is. Instead of fighting tae kwon do experts or gangs of skillful kung fu fighters, Chan merely throws around a bunch of sluggish, professional wrestler types.

The Big Brawl did give Chan the opportunity to appear on numerous American talk shows, such as *The Mike Douglas Show, That's Incredible,* and *Today.* Appearing with Christopher Reeve and Melissa Gilbert on *The Mike Douglas Show,* Chan's lack of English had no apparent effect on his natural, good sense of humor. When Mike Douglas asked him if he stayed in contact with his parents, Chan replied that his parents would send him letters with money in it. "Well, didn't you miss them?" Douglas persisted. "Ah, I miss the letter!" Chan quickly rejoined. The audience roared in laughter, but before they could settle back down in their chairs, Douglas asked Chan if he could swat a fly that came into sight. Chan pretended to swoop up the fly, and before Douglas can say another thing, he mimicked throwing it into his mouth. If anything, Chan made people laugh, and this sense of comedy was his only defense against the "martial arts actor" label. The show ended with Chan performing a freestyle kata (a practice form in martial arts composed of pre-scribed movements) and teaching Douglas the one-inch punch. On *That's Incredible*, he per-formed the same routine, and all of the ques-tioning had to do with comparing Chinese food and women to American.

Chan would next appear in two *Cannonball Run* films made in 1981 and 1983. "I remember totaling up the costs for the cars and the actors and finding that I needed more money," said director Hal Needham. Needham met with Golden Harvest and arranged for the films to be made as coproductions, giving Chan yet another opportunity to find an audience in America.

In the first film, Chan and Michael Hui, Golden Harvest's comic sensation, play a pair of Japanese car drivers who enter the competition.

The purpose of the film was to showcase as many stars as possible, such as Burt Reynolds, Farrah Fawcett, and Dean Martin, and let off a series of sight gags and jokes within a loose structure. Needham had heard of Chan but knew nothing of what he could really do, and with such an orgy of stars, Chan and Hui need-ed to do more than just make their presence known. After seeing Chan demonstrate his agili-ty for the first time, Needham agreed to let him pretty much run his fight the way he wanted. *Almost* the way he wanted: Chan couldn't con-vince Needham to let him have a month-long shoot! In his fight, Chan has a couple of moments, most notably with motorcycle gang member Peter Fonda. Without the time to detail the fight choreography, however, Chan comes off as being just another guy who can throw a kick.

Nevertheless, Chan meshed well with the Hollywood stars. In a documentary on

Chan's only substantive scene in *The Cannonball Run* was fighting a few bikers led by Peter Fonda. (*By permission of Media Asia Group. © STAR TV*)

Cannonball Run, Burt Reynolds commented, "I think he's one picture away from being a legend like Bruce [Lee] was." A dialogue coach would go over every line with Chan, since his English speaking ability was still lacking "Most of my actors would spend their time in their trailers if they weren't in a scene," recalled Needham, "but Jackie would be hanging around the set, trying to learn everything he could about how we do things in America."

    Cannonball Run did fairly well in America but met with a lukewarm response in Hong Kong. However, the Japanese market took very well to the film, so Golden Harvest opted to use Chan for the sequel. The emphasis was on big stars and fast cars, though, and Chan barely set foot out of his superinjected vehicle, where he was paired up with Richard Kiel, "Jaws" of James Bond fame. Given little to do, Chan was just another face on the screen. There were two short martial arts sequences, but everyone beats up the bad guys—including Dom DeLuise in a superhero costume!

    In between the two *Cannonball Run* starfests, Chan would return to Hong Kong and mark his first real effort in what would be the Jackie Chan genre. The film industry there was still clinging to the very late Ching Dynasty, setting virtually all kung fu films in the late 1800s to early 1900s. Unable to truly break out of the period mold, Chan's effort was called at first *Young Master in Love*, a rather melodramatic title that was later changed to *Dragon Lord*. The uneven script once again focuses on relationships while tugging at traditional values.

    As the son in a rich family, Dragon (Chan) has virtually no responsibilities except for learning from various tutors imposed by his strict father. He pays no attention and opts for chasing girls and competing in bizarre sporting events with his cousin Cowboy, who's given this nickname because his father's import business

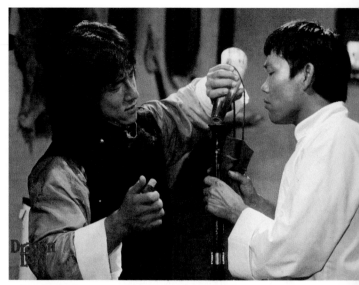

A film about friendship: *Dragon Lord*. Cowboy is played by longtime stuntman and friend Mars. (*Colin Geddes/Asian Eye. By permission of Media Asia Group. © STAR TV*)

centers on Western culture. The film's initial premise of love superseding friendship quickly disappears when Chan stumbles upon a band of thieves scheming to sell China's ancient treasures for profit. Chan doesn't really see a problem with this until he befriends one of the thieves, who wants to put a stop to them. After three skirmishes with the group, Chan once again faces Whang Inn-sik, who plays the chief of the group.

    Despite the setting and the costumes, *Dragon Lord* has nothing to do with martial arts nor anything that would appear in Chan's earlier kung fu films. "The story focuses on the relationships with his friends, sort of an ode to his Peking Opera days," says screenwriter Edward Tang. "Friendship and competition has a very interesting bond, and I wanted to bring this out into the open." By focusing on typical problems with friendship and love, the action sequences aren't rigid tests of fighting ability but natural tests of physical ability. Each scene in the film is a set piece instead of just another fight.

    The opening action scene is a "king of the mountain" exhibition, with groups of young men climbing to the top of a forty-foot structure to claim a golden egg. Once back on the ground, the person with the egg must fight his

The "King of the Mountain" competition. (*Colin Geddes/Asian Eye. By permission of Media Asia Group. © STAR TV*)

Chan goes for the golden egg. (*By permission of Media Asia Group. © STAR TV*)

(*By permission of Media Asia Group. © STAR TV*)

way to his table and place the egg inside of a pouch. "We had over ninety stuntmen in that scene, and everyone got hurt," remembers Tai Po, who played one of Chan's youthful friends. Chan's direction shows off these wiry stuntmen executing kicks, flips, and flops to obtain the egg in breathtaking wide angle shots.

The finale of the second action sequence has been etched into Chan's résumé as containing the shot requiring the greatest number of takes. Chan is participating in a sort of soccer game, the players moving a shuttlecock back and forth like a Hacky Sack, using knees, feet, arms, heads, and any other body part to knock the feathered cork into the net. The game begins to look bad for Chan's opponents, whose missed kick gives him the opportunity to win the game by kicking the shuttlecock some thirty feet into their net.

The audience clearly sees Chan performing this feat. Since the majority of the game is left in wide shots with few cuts, timing and coordination had to be in perfect synch to make this last shot work. It boggles the mind to think how long it must have taken to shoot, for all the complex plays to work and Chan's incredible game-winner to go in. What the audience doesn't know is that it took one thousand attempts to get it right!

When Chan cleverly tries to send his love a let-

Chan didn't learn his lesson in *Dragon Lord,* so here he is again, fighting Whang Inn-sik. (*Colin Geddes/Asian Eye. By permission of Media Asia Group. © STAR TV*)

ter via kite, the wind carries it to the roof of the bad guys. Before he can snatch it back, the roof scene becomes yet another set piece, with Chan hopping around to avoid a series of well-placed spears that come crashing up through the shingles. In some instances, Chan would barely rise up from the roof, just barely being missed by the tip of a spear—all without quick editing, a further example of breakneck timing. Shortly thereafter, Chan tries once again to talk with his love but is interrupted by two of the thieves, who push him to the edge. Jumping through wooden fixtures, climbing up columns, and literally running up the wall to clown around with his foes, Chan shows his intricate choreography to be more playful than the normal, structured fighting of his previous film efforts.

Dragon Lord represents Chan's new direction of bringing action to the screen, and the finale can be said to give the first taste of what makes a Jackie Chan fight sequence so compelling to watch. When Whang beats up Cowboy and asserts his fancy footwork on

Chan, there is an excitement that quickly burns every other Chan fight scene before it. During the entire film Whang's face is somewhat blocked by other variables on the screen until his duel with Chan, when the camera jump zooms in on the fact that one of his eyes is completely white! By giving the villain extra flavor, the fight starts rather abruptly. Inside of a feed mill Chan runs at his opponent without any type of formal movements, just swinging arms and feet.

Of course, Chan undergoes rather than inflicts more punishment until they get to the second story of the mill. In a unique form of obsession, Chan is determined to knock Whang to the ground below. At one point, he is standing on the outside of a railing and tugging at Whang relentlessly, even though getting his wish would mean he would fall, too.

The scene is important because it shows that Chan's action character is not immune to punishment but merely accepts it as part of the job. In one amazing shot, Chan is kicked to the ground below, only to land right on top of Cowboy, played by Mars. "Jackie and I both went to the hospital with bruised backs," recalled Mars in thinking back to the scene. The most amazing highlight is when Chan jumps down a feed chute and kicks Whang a dozen feet away. Doubling for Whang, a stuntman stood idly by on top of a bag of grain and let Chan push-kick him. An elaborate pulley effect propels the stuntman into the air, where he performs a backflip before flopping to the ground. Chan immediately jumps on his back, then leaps onto stacked bags of grain, and does a backflip, landing on Whang's back again! As if that wasn't enough, Chan smothers Whang with more grain

(*By permission of Media Asia Group. © STAR TV*)

bags until he's finished off. The mixture of realistic fighting and amazing stuntwork denotes the classic Jackie Chan action scene, and this feed mill sequence was the first.

For *Dragon Lord* Chan added two more men to his team of stuntmen, dubbed Sing Kar Pan, known to the rest of the world as Jackie's Stunt Team. One of them, Cheung Wing-fat, first met Chan in 1967 during his own tour of duty in a Peking Opera school. It was a regular practice for students of different schools to mingle and discuss the tricks of the trade. Cheung and Chan became good friends, and Cheung found work with the Shaw Brothers like many other young opera students of his age. Audiences wouldn't know him by the name Cheung, since he adopted Fwa Sing as his Chinese stage name, which translates to Mars in English. He assumed the oddball name Mars because he thought it fit his oddball facial features. "Mars is the comedian of the group, and he always has a joke to tell on the set," said Tai Po. Mars also serves on the committee for the Hong Kong Suntman Association and has worked with Chan on nearly every single film since, as well as contributing to Sammo Hung's films (although in recent years, he has worked solely as a stuntman).

Since *Dragon Lord* was shot in Taipei, Taiwan (the original location was Seoul, Korea, but it proved too cold), Chan got to see many different stuntmen in action, and from them he added Benny Lai Keung-kuen to the group. Although he can be seen in *Dragon Lord, Police Story,* and *Mr. Canton and Lady Rose,* Lai is best known to audiences as the animalistic, mute fighter who tangles with Chan in the climax of *Police Story II.*

Dragon Lord was Chan's decisive move toward more Westernized ways, leaving much of the Chinese culture to simply blend into the background. The Cowboy character is an obvious signal; he and Chan are hunting with Western guns when they come across the film's thieves. Chan seems more concerned with meeting girls, playing with his friends, and just plain goofing off than meeting his Chinese obligations as a son.

Chan's character doesn't seem to care about Chinese history or even the preservation of rare artifacts, which is what the thieves are stealing. (Chan came up with the idea of artifact theft while running through the many plot synopses at Golden Harvest.)

But what about kung fu? In the beginning of *Dragon Lord,* Chan performs a few freestyle kung fu forms under his father's watchful eye. Anything honoring his heritage, in fact, is done just to please his father. The audience can see that Chan is adept at martial arts, yet he can't seem to use any of it when faced with a violent situation, where Chan trades in the formalized movements of kung fu for his acrobatic fighting skills.

As evidence that the original script was completely devoid of the artifact plot, the last shot has Chan and Mars holding up an inscribed banner that reads, "I won't love girls anymore"—as if this was a lesson to be learned about the pitfalls of friendship. *Dragon Lord* would have been quite a different film if it had kept to the original story without the fight sequence at the end.

Dragon Lord did very poorly in Hong Kong, but it proved to have the necessary staying power for the Japanese market as well as internationally. Chan's new take on fight choreography did not win the Best Action Design award at the first annual Hong Kong Film Awards. Instead, critics gave the award to Sammo Hung for his work on the groundbreaking wing chun film *The Prodigal Son.* With all of the essential ingredients in place and a need to move his self-created genre into a modern setting, this was Chan's final period film until *Drunken Master II* twelve years later—when he again uses theft of Chinese artifacts as the film's premise.

✳

In 1985, three years after *Dragon Lord,* Chan was ready to try another starring role as an American action star. Although the *Cannonball Run* films were popular around the world, Chan had only a small piece of the action. He yearned for American stardom—but not in a period piece like *The Big Brawl* or with a bit part as in

The Protector (1985). *(By permission of Media Asia Group.
© STAR TV)*

Cannonball Run. Impressed with his previous work, a Golden Harvest producer felt that James Glickenhaus could give American audiences the Chan they were supposed to know. Based on a script by Robert Clouse, *The Protector* is a modern-day action vehicle appropriate for Charles Bronson, Clint Eastwood, and—Glickenhaus apparently thought—Jackie Chan. The film is everything that Chan isn't, but it's a great film for analysis because Chan re-edited it and shot new footage for its release in Hong Kong. The comparisons between the two are astonishing.

Director Glickenhaus understood Jackie Chan, or so he thought. He knew about Chan's martial arts skills and his use of comedy in keeping violence out of the action, but Glickenhaus was an established director of B-grade action flicks like *The Exterminator.* His style was pedestrian Hollywood filmmaking, and his script for *The Protector* was typical of his work. Aside from shooting Chan as if he were Charles Bronson, the main differences between Glickenhaus's American *Protector* and Chan's Hong Kong version are the male-orient-

ed characteristics Hollywood has given the action genre, including nudity, foul language, bloodletting, and male bonding. The American version contains all of these attributes, with Chan playing a New York cop who gets in trouble with the force, only to be teamed up with a new partner, played by Danny Aiello. When the host of a fashion show they are attending is kidnapped, Chan and Aiello are sent to Hong Kong following a hot tip. The kidnapping turns out to be nothing more than the move of a pawn set in a larger game between two drug lords fighting for control.

Chan and Glickenhaus did not get along on the set, and the experience left him in dismay as to whether he could make it in America or not. On several occasions Glickenhaus would let his assistants take over while he stayed in his trailer. Even with this kind of mishandling, no one would listen to Chan, who had his own ideas on how the action had to be filmed. With his hands tied, Chan merely performed the movements Glickenhaus wanted until the latter returned to the States.

With the chance to recut the film for the Asian market, Chan enlisted Aiello and martial artist Bill "Superfoot" Wallace to reshoot the ending as well as film additional scenes. Expletives are common in standard action fare, so Chan resubtitled the film with whatever he

The Protector. (*Colin Geddes/Asian Eye. By permission of Media Asia Group. © STAR TV*)

The big motorcycle jump in *The Protector*. (*Colin Geddes/Asian Eye. By permission of Media Asia Group. © STAR TV*)

wanted. So when tough guy Chan has to use tough guy language, like "Give me the fuckin' keys!," Chan merely changes it to "Give me the keys!" American slang was also excised from the Asian cut of the film for obvious reasons.

And what exploitive action flick would be complete without a little "T 'n' A"? You won't find any in a Jackie Chan movie, though (except for the occasional comic shot of Chan's derrière). When Chan and Aiello first arrive in Hong Kong, they are led to a massage parlor for information. The American version includes a strip scene and several sexual innuendoes, all of which are perfunctory devices to set up a fight. Chan cuts all of this from the Asian print. The most gratuitous scene is the final onslaught on the drug bosses' operation, where four female workers are completely naked. Many drug operations do make their employees work in the nude to prevent stealing, but it's absurd to think that *The Protector* or any other action film would try to adhere to anything realistic. Chan cuts every shot of nudity from the film, even shooting new footage of a fully clothed actress mixing heroin for the sake of continuity.

The main difference between the two versions, however, is in the action. Chan adds three action scenes and retools the final fight to the standards set by his Hong Kong films.

Furthermore, Edward Tang was brought in

to clean up the American version, and he added two additional subplots to create more action, making the film more interesting. The Chan character brings a mysterious Chinese coin to Hong Kong in search of a link to the kidnapping. The Asian version makes better use of this device as it pairs Chan up with Hong Kong singer-actress Sally Yeh, who plays the daughter of the deceased owner of the coin. In their initial meeting, which takes place in a dance studio, Chan has a brief fight in a connecting gym with two of the studio's dancers. Yeh's character is soon able to explain much of the convolution unresolved in the American version, and she also sets up a second action sequence, which takes place in her apartment. It isn't much: Chan must diffuse a bomb and shoot an intruder at the door.

The American version contains a strain of plotting that deals with a kindly, old Chinese merchant who is connected to the coin and to the Hong Kong drug lord. When Chan and Aiello quiz him on the whereabouts of the kidnapped girl, he says he will find out. He is killed thirty minutes later—gruesomely impaled to a burning ship in which he does business. The merchant's daughter is left to blame Chan for his death.

In Chan's hands, this is yet another chance to add a fight scene. Chan took every opportunity to add some pizzazz to the original film. The Asian version brings the merchant to meet a contact in a harbor, but he is interrupted by the drug bosses' men and Wallace. Chan's stuntman Fong Hak-on is clearly seen, and Wallace gets a chance to show off the karate skills that made him famous in the ring (Wallace had earlier played Chuck Norris's nemesis in *A Force of One*). Chan and the merchant's daughter then show up to meet the contact, as well, only to find her father and the contact left for dead. The daughter's reaction is much more severe, and it gives Chan more reason to put a stop to the drug lord's activities.

As a side note, Moon Lee, who played the merchant's daughter, could not deliver her lines well enough in English, and the Chinese dubbing proved to make her scenes stronger. She would become one of the biggest female martial arts stars in Hong Kong just two years later with *Angel*, after receiving extensive training.

The most interesting differences between the American and Chinese versions is in the final fight between Chan and Bill Wallace. The Glickenhaus version is rather short, considering it was supposed to be a classic matchup, and it's shot in typical Hollywood fashion. Wallace throws a kick, Chan blocks; Chan throws a punch, Wallace throws another kick; and so on.

Understanding real combat, Chan runs his version quite a bit differently. The choreography is more intricate, with numerous blows exchanged from both sides at once. Although Chan uses some of the original footage, he adds the showy acrobatics that have made him the star he is today. The most memorable moments come when Chan is fighting Wallace next to a

Hong Kong newspaper ad, which shows Sally Yeh. (*Colin Geddes/Asian Eye. By permission of Media Asia Group. © STAR TV*)

steel fence. In one shot, Chan clings to the fence, does a backward flip over Wallace, and pulls him over the top. Then, seen from a different angle, Chan is kicked into the fence, bounces off of it, and powers right back at Wallace in one incredible take! It's this kind of artistry that Hollywood doesn't understand.

Other comparisons of the two versions' fight choreography, direction, and editing reveal vastly different cuts of the film, and Chan's cut easily comes out ahead. After winning in the early going of the fight, Wallace comes back with a buzz saw. The original version is shot with nice, wide angles that reveal Wallace's slowness and lack of maneuverability with the saw. Chan reshot the sequence, adding quick cuts to speed up the action and give it the intensity that it needs. Chan's version also includes the more accented sound effects for kicks and punches, compared to the realism of the American cut. Glickenhaus openly admitted to shooting the film with masters, which he backed up with different shots. One master shot of Chan kneeing an opponent in the face was so bad (his knee doesn't even come close!) that Chan just takes the sequence out altogether. Also, Glickenhaus generally didn't want to speed up the film, but there are several instances where he does speed up part of a shot. This exposes the technique to the audience, when the fast section is sandwiched between sections at regular speed!

If *The Protector* had had a lighter tone like the one in *The Big Brawl* it might have been bearable. Instead, it unforgivingly turns Chan into a stone-faced "action hero," really bringing to light his big nose and misuse of the English language as he delivers serious lines.

The Protector soured Chan on Hollywood: he has gone on record in Hong Kong declaring that he doesn't care about the American market anymore. But the desire for American success and stardom was merely dormant—it couldn't die, not in a man who can't walk away from a challenge. It would take almost a decade for Jackie Chan to be a household name in America.

The Three Kung-fu-teers

Jackie Chan, Sammo Hung, and Yuen Biao

When America thinks of its great comic trios, the Marx brothers and the Three Stooges come to mind. Staging physical sight gags in uniquely absurd comic structures, each trio member created his own individual persona and bounced that energy off the others. The audience doesn't know whom to watch if they are all on the screen, and they can't make up their minds whom they like better.

To Asian audiences Jackie Chan, Sammo Hung, and Yuen Biao can be called the kung fu fighting Marx Brothers, a trio of colorful and not entirely conventional heroes. Just by looking at them, to think that they were action movie protagonists would almost seem to be a joke. With a thick mop top and big nose, Jackie is the tallest of the group at 5 feet 9 inches and 154 pounds. Yuen Biao, with his unmistakable mole and jagged teeth, stands only 5 feet 6 inches and weighs 150 pounds. More puzzling to the eye is Sammo, the rotund 220-pound member, who looks even more out of place at 5 feet 8 inches. The American film industry would have literally laughed actors with these statistics off the lot, but they all bring to the table something that American action stars can't. The trio represents commonplace, run-of-the mill people—the same people who go and watch these movies in the first place. In identifying with the person on the screen, the viewer thinks that he or she has what it takes to become a hero.

And true heroes are proof of the potential of the ordinary person. In the Peking Opera school, Sammo Hung became "Big Brother" since he was the oldest, born January 7, 1952. Unlike many of the other students, Hung (known

Japanese ad slick for *Winners & Sinners* (*The Five Lucky Stars* in Japan). (*Colin Geddes/Asian Eye*)

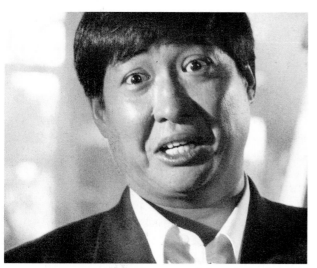

Sammo Hung in *Dragons Forever.* *(Colin Geddes/Asian Eye.*
By permission of Media Asia Group. © STAR TV)

as Chu Yuen Lung) wanted to be a part of the
school, noting all of the skills he would learn.
He often taught the class when Master Yu was
away. Both of his parents were in the film business, and he was mainly cared for at first by his
grandparents. Hung was an adventurous youth,
so it wasn't too hard for them to let him go (to
opera school) at the age of ten. One year later
Hung found his first acting role in *Education of
Love,* and by 1968 he was ready for action films.

Hung was no stranger to action. As a
sprawling teenager in his Peking Opera school
days, he often got into fights. Once Hung and
friend went to a local disco where he began
showing off for a group of girls by performing
back flips. Some of the other boys at the disco
were jealous, and when Hung ventured outside,
they jumped him. The result of the fight literally
scarred him for life: on the top of Hung's upper
lip is the clear impression of a pop bottle. This
experience and others is a probable influence on
Hung's brutal, street-brawling style of screen
action later.

At the tender age of sixteen, Hung starred
as a Japanese swordsman in the popular sword-
play film *A Touch of Zen.* With the formation of
Golden Harvest, Hung joined their ranks in 1971
with *The Fast Sword* and quickly built up a
resume as a worthy fight choreographer and
minor supporting player. Out of all the Peking

Opera brothers, Hung was the first to really
make a career in films.

Hung has often said that he created kung fu
comedy with his directorial debut, *The Iron-
Fisted Monk,* which was released the same year
as *Snake in the Eagle's Shadow,* 1978. Hardly a
comedy, it does have many of the elements that
also make Chan's kung fu comedies work, and
the scripting and fight choreography were top-
notch, compared with normal fare. According
to Hung, he wanted Chan for *The Iron-Fisted
Monk,* but Chan was living in Australia at the
time. It's interesting to speculate how Chan's
career might have been affected if he had started
with this film instead of *Snake in the Eagle's
Shadow.* Hung's other early kung fu features
were more original and entertaining than Chan's
Lo Wei films because he had control over the
productions; in time, in fact, he would grow to
be one of Golden Harvest's most trusted producers.

The eighties was the decade of change for
Hong Kong cinema, unleashing fresh, "New
Wave" directors whose passions gave life to the
stagnant cinema they'd inherited from the mid-
seventies. The film that brought attention to
these New Wave directors was *Aces Go Places*
(1981), launching Cinema City (partly founded
by Dean Shek, Chan's comic foe in the Seasonal
films) as the new kid on the block. With major
production values and colorful, large-scale
stunts, *Aces Go Places* became Hong Kong's first
big franchise film, with two sequels churned out
over the next two years, among others that followed in the mold. Adjusting box office receipts
for inflation (among other variables), these
three *Aces* films are the three biggest money-
makers of all time in Hong Kong.

Just two years later Golden Harvest set new
standards for special effects with New Wave
director Tsui Hark's *ZU: Warriors of the Magic
Mountain* and established a franchise of its own,
the *Lucky Stars* films—a brainchild of Hung's.
Sammo Hung and Yuen Biao both appeared in
ZU, but Hung's involvement with the *Lucky
Stars* series would lead to a major success with
Golden Harvest. In fact, *My Lucky Stars* and
Twinkle, Twinkle Lucky Stars hold the fourth and

In the center stand Benny Urquidez and Keith Vitali, two of America's top martial artists, who lent their expertise to fight scenes in *Wheels on Meals*. (*Colin Geddes/Asian Eye. By permission of Media Asia Group. © STAR TV*)

Some of the most brilliant sequences in the film stem from Chan's job as a waiter, gliding to and fro through Barcelona's crowded streets via skateboard with orders of food. One would think that most of Chan's and Yuen's skateboard work was doubled, but the end credit sequence on the Japanese version shows the two practicing, with plenty of hard knocks to prove any doubters wrong.

Unlike *Project A*, it's share and share alike in *Wheels on Meals*. Chan isn't given the chance to upstage Yuen's talents, and vice versa. Hung pretty much leaves things to his two junior brothers except for the end, where the three must fence off against the lead villain with swords. "All for one, and one for all," they say in the Chinese equivalent. With moments like this, it's a shame that the three didn't make more films like *Wheels on Meals*—a light, colorful vehicle filled with action and great scenery.

As for the odd title, it was originally *Meals on Wheels,* but a Golden Harvest representative, noting bad luck with films whose titles started with M, switched the two words just before it was released. In Japan they didn't bother with either title, calling the film *Spartan X.*

In *Return of the Dragon*, Bruce Lee ventured beyond Hong Kong to shoot in Rome, which gave the film a fresher look. The end fight served as a reminder of the ancient gladiators, except that Lee and Chuck Norris were using feet and fists instead of swords. Hong Kong doesn't provide filmmakers the luxury of much variation in set designs—it just isn't possible, due to the lack of space. Sammo Hung was the first director to entice Chan from the Asian locales that he had always called home in his Hong Kong films. Barcelona's architecture and stunning vistas gave *Wheels on Meals* an international touch, as does a European love interest.

Wheels on Meals was also Chan's first Hong Kong film to bring non-Asian fighters to tangle with him and Yuen. Keith Vitali and Benny "the Jet" Urquidez added a harder edge to the fight sequences, something beyond the showy kung fu matchups. Vitali was a former American karate champion during the late seventies, and Urquidez was an undefeated kickboxing champion, fighting all over the world and claiming a large following in Hong Kong and Japan. The latter was noted as the most popular American martial artist in Japan and was even featured in a comic book showing many of his real-life ring moves. For good reason, too: in 1977 Urquidez was the first American ever to win a karate championship in Japan against a Japanese.

While promoting a documentary that he had produced, Urquidez was contacted by the Golden Harvest office, asking him if he wanted to work with Chan. He really didn't know who Jackie Chan was at the time, but he saw the script and agreed to star in the film. Vitali got a call from American fight choreographer Pat Johnson *(The Big Brawl)*, who asked him if he was interested in working with Chan. The only stipulation was that he had to make up his mind in two days! Soon Vitali and Urquidez were on a plane to Barcelona for a rough-and-

Chan and Urquidez rest between bouts. (*Courtesy of Sara Urquidez*)

While the end fight between Urquidez and Chan was one of the best fight scenes ever filmed, it was also one of the most controversial. During the filming of the movie, rumors spread that the two really did not like each other and that Chan was steamed over Urquidez's inability to pull his punches. In fact, they were both hitting each other for real, but more on that later. It was said that Chan had even challenged Urquidez to a real fight.

 At first the hostility was thought of as a joke. Soon, though, all of the other actors and stuntmen were making bets around the set, increasing the likelihood of a real match taking place. Vitali clearly remembers the two getting a bit miffed at each other, though neither one ever really showed it.

Chan's being an actor, hiding the pain was not as important as it was to a real fighter like Urquidez. Perhaps it was a show of face to the Chinese crew—or the aggressive atmosphere—that created these flared tensions. Nonetheless, Chan's pride kept the true extent of the punishment concealed from the cast and crew.

All this created excitement, both for the crew and for the screen results, but it was not entirely genuine hostility, according to Urquidez. Here's Benny's account of the challenge to put on a real fight exhibition:

'"Look, Jackie, do you really want to do this exhibition?'

He said, 'Sure, I really want to do it.'

'Now, I want you to understand that I am a professional fighter, and when I do an exhibition, I'm kicking and hitting for real.'

'I understand,' Chan said.

'No playing like this. I know that this is showbiz and we control certain things, but in the ring—that's a different story.'

'I know, I know,' Jackie replied.

Kidding, of course, I began saying to Jackie, 'I hope you are ready for this—you had better start doing your jumping jacks and your sit-ups, because I throw one mean spinning back kick.'

'Oh yeah?!' Jackie exclaimed. 'I can jump so high that you can't kick me!'

'Well, Jackie, they don't call me "the Jet" for nothing!'

I knew in my heart that we weren't really going to fight, but it was something that we could just rib each other about. It made us feel good amid all of the punishment that both of us endured shooting that final scene."

At the outcome of the *Wheels on Meals* fight, Urquidez says to Chan, "Okay, we'll have one more match, one more match." What truly happened may never be completely revealed, but Urquidez and Chan have remained close friends ever since. On-screen the two would pair up again four years later in *Dragons Forever*.

(*Courtesy of Sara Urquidez*)

Left to right: Eric Tsang, Sibelle Hu, Richard Ng, Sammo Hung, Charlie Chin, and Stanley Fong in *My Lucky Stars*. (*Colin Geddes/Asian Eye*)

tumble lesson in Hong Kong film fighting.

Chan sat down both budding action stars and showed them several of his films, explaining the differences in choreography between America and Asia. There were other things, however, that they had to learn for themselves. In one scene Vitali had to perform a spin kick and break a spear that Hung was holding. He went through two suits because of the sweat and over thirty-five takes. "I was getting restless, and I spun around as hard as I could, not only breaking the spear but knocking Hung out in the process with a blow to the head. The set was quiet, and I thought I was fired for knocking the director unconscious! After a few seconds, Hung stood up, hugged me, and spoke to the crew in Chinese. Essentially, Hung had earned his red badge of courage, noting that if he could take this kind of punishment, so could everyone else."

In 1985 Sammo Hung rejuvenated the *Winners & Sinners* formula by bringing the team to Japan in *My Lucky Stars*. Without Sham back for the sequel, though, Eric Tsang would be his replacement. This is the best of the series overall, and it became Golden Harvest's biggest

money-maker of all time (adjusting for inflation and other factors). It has more action and a cohesive plot-line. Chan is given more of a supporting role and, best of all, more fighting time.

At the very beginning cops Chan and Yuen follow two criminals (Lam Ching-ying and Lau Kar-wing) to an amusement park bustling with activity, only to be trapped by ninjas who kidnap Yuen. For some reason Chan contacts his police superior in Hong Kong and asks for the help of the Lucky Stars to bring the criminals to justice and rescue Yuen. Again the five are assembled and blackmailed to come to Chan's aid in Japan. The superior's assistant, played by Hu, accompanies the group, leading to an onslaught of more comedy centered around earning her affections. Of course, it doesn't work, so the group's only purpose is spouting off lines of Cantonese humor.

What's lost in the translation is of no concern to Western audiences, since the action is the real star in this film. After a worthy encounter—Chan and Hung fighting off a bunch of masked villains—the real treat takes place in the amusement park's maze of horrors. After Chan, dressed in a cartoonish costume, faces a samurai warrior, he makes his way through the darkness punching, kicking, and shooting at several odd entities that catch him off guard. Chan fights Dick Wei for a second time, and Hung battles Shaw Brothers veteran Lau Kar-wing. The set pieces are colorful and imaginative, and the film unsurprisingly did very well in the Japanese market.

The third film in the series, *Twinkle, Twinkle Lucky Stars* (1985), is a complete mess. It probably wouldn't make a difference how many times one viewed it—the plot doesn't make a glimmer of sense. "We were told to get that one finished within a month and a half from begin-

Chan meets Dick Wei again in the explosive warehouse
fight of *Twinkle, Twinkle Lucky Stars*. (*Colin Geddes/Asian
Eye*)

that just doesn't translate. The English-dubbed version is so bad, in fact, that it is recommended that one only see the fight scenes—everything else is garbage. The actors' characters changed once again, Hu is now a police detective who summons the gang to help foil a trio of assassins bent on killing a drug boss in Hong Kong. Replacing Hu, Rosamund Kwan becomes the sex object for the gang to hit on in the same fashion as in the previous film.

Thankfully, Jackie Chan and Yuen Biao are in even more of a supporting role this time out, and their skills are put to good use in several fight sequences. In the first scene, which has nothing to do with the plot of the film, Chan, Yuen Biao, and up-and-coming star Andy Lau take on a warehouse of Hung regulars, including Dick Wei, Chin Kar-lok, and Philip Ko Fei. When a car chase ensues later on, Chan goes head to head with Richard Norton, ending with Norton getting the upper hand. The finale was supposed to pit the two against each other in a rematch, but Chan's back injury from the simultaneously shot *Police Story* prevented that from taking place.

Chan bows out of the would-be rematch early, spotlighting Hung, who comes to his rescue and defeats Norton. The comedy in the film may have been wasted, but international audiences finally got to see what Hung could do as a martial artist. He fights a group of crossdressing killers in the beginning of the film, beats Norton to a pulp, and finally engages Kurata with a pair of tennis rackets in probably the best gag of the whole film. "When I got back to my hotel room from shooting that scene with Sammo," said Richard Norton of the dizzying experience, "I said to myself, 'If I can get through this, I can get through anything.'" The other great highlight of the film is when Yuen Biao executes a cartwheel off of a crate, throws a roundhouse kick, followed by a perfect side kick.

Several *Lucky Stars* installments were made

ning to end," commented Richard Ng. "As it usually happens in Hong Kong, everything is backdated: We decide on a release date, and then we have to come up with the day the movie has to be finished by."

Luckily, *Twinkle, Twinkle Lucky Stars* is more action-packed than the two previous *Lucky Stars* films combined, and again Hung tries for a more international approach, setting the film in Thailand. He also creates a little cultural diversity, with the three villains played by Australian martial artist Richard Norton, Japanese veteran bad guy Shoji Kurata, and Hung regular Chung Fat. Pat Johnson recommended Richard Norton to Chan as being a potential fighter in a Hong Kong production. To Norton, the experience of filming the final fight between Hung and him "was the hardest thing, initially, that I can think of in terms of film. We were shooting in the Golden Harvest studios with no air conditioning, and the temperature would sometimes get up to 115 degrees!"

While the sight gags and universal Cantonese humor in the first two films seemed to work for non-Asian audiences, *Twinkle, Twinkle Lucky Stars* suffers from absurd gags lifted from the previous films and verbal humor shortly thereafter without the benefit of Chan or Yuen. Hung would play in some of them, even when the series was abandoned by Golden Harvest and featured a whole new batch of younger players. The *Aces Go Places* series started to dwindle as well, so it was only natural that a combination film would be released entitled *Lucky Stars Go Places* (1987).

Hong Kong films have often been categorized as mixed bags since they tend to throw in a little bit of everything, hoping to try and please everyone at the same time. Typically, a film will stick to one particular base, say comedy, then build around it with straight dramatic sequences and action. Critics often chastise films like this, calling them uneven, but this is perhaps the one quality that keeps audiences interested, never knowing how the film will turn out.

Sammo Hung can arguably be called the best "uneven" director around, although he has proven himself time and time again with balanced efforts. He had used his crews made up of martial arts stars and stuntmen in various straight action and kung fu films. In Hong Kong during the late eighties, though, every type of ensemble was devised, from groups of kids to teams of female detectives, so our trio needed to try something that even they weren't sure could work: hard-core drama. Hung's 1985 film *Heart*

of Dragon is a compelling story of two brothers, Hung and Chan, with the regular crew as background players. This ambitious effort is a somber story with unnerving, brutal violence—and with none of Chan's usual light-hearted touches. "I needed a break from fighting all the time, so I came up with an idea for a drama," said Hung in a recent interview on the set of *Once Upon a Time in China & America*. Hung's regular screenwriter, Barry Wong, best known for penning John Woo's *The Killer* and *Hard-boiled*, was called in for this script.

Hung starts the film with a quick action sequence so that the film's human drama won't be interrupted later. He stages a mock exhibition of warfare between members of a Chinese SWAT team including Chan. Chan's life is a never-ending juggling act: he's tired of being a cop, wants to be with his girlfriend, and dreams of working on a ship to see the world. Only one thing truly holds him back—his retarded brother. Even with his boyish face, childish attire, and bowl haircut, Hung still looks like a man, but he has the intelligence of a kid. His ambition is to do whatever kids do, including going to a local restaurant, where his companions trick him into posing as a parent to buy ice cream for everyone.

In Hollywood *Rain Man* (1988) exhibited some real emotions, but the device-driven characters kept the film operatic and sensationalized. Tom Cruise had to prove to himself that the relationship with his brother was more important than money, and Dustin Hoffman had this paradoxical mental condition giving him certain extraordinary skills but depriving him of brainpower for everything else. The film provided lots of laughs to keep mainstream audiences happy, and it made its point about caring for the mentally ill.

By contrast, in *Heart of Dragon* Hung keeps the human qualities intact, without diluting them with caustic humor. They are reflected in simple actions unscathed by overacting or unrealistic scripting.

Heart of Dragon (1985). (*Colin Geddes/Asian Eye. By permission of Media Asia Group. © STAR TV*)

Hong Kong newspaper ad for *Heart of Dragon*. (*Colin Geddes/Asian Eye. By permission of Media Asia Group. © STAR TV*)

A little bit of sappiness is inserted for good measure.

Chan plays an unlikable, selfish wreck who cares for Hung, his slow brother, but doesn't feel the need to let that compassion be known to the rest of the world. In one scene Chan and Hung are walking down the street holding hands, mainly so Chan can keep control of Hung's childish curiosity. When people begin laughing, even to the point of calling the hand-holding homosexual, Chan merely points to Hung and repeats the line "He's my brother" over and over again. In one of the most poignant scenes in the film, Hung's tutor dehumanizes him with remarks about his intelligence and plight in life. Chan hears all this from outside the door, and waits awhile before running in and throwing the tutor out. He believes that what the tutor is saying is the truth and doesn't immediately try to intervene. He accepts his brother, but treats him more like a chore that's simply part of a routine.

The interesting script touches on the hypocrisy of Chan's actions. After Chan saves Hung from extended embarrassment, the following scene shows Chan with his hands over his ears and his back turned while his SWAT team friend lectures him about the fragility of his brother. But it's easy for someone to chastise

him for not caring for Hung. After all, the friend doesn't have to put up with Hung day in and day out. And the whole time, Hung is touchingly seen sitting on the couch as if he had done something wrong.

Heart of Dragon never lets an ounce of unwanted comedy enter the picture, and Chan looks so natural as a dramatic lead that one would hardly be able to tell that he was known for comedic performances. The best scene in the entire film brings all of the emotions out into the open as Chan and Hung go head to head with heated dialogue. In one sequence Chan says that he sometimes wishes that Hung were dead, while putting his hands around Hung's neck and shaking him violently. To end the sequence a brilliant move of the camera focuses on Chan, his hands over his eyes in despair, then pans to the left and zooms in on Hung, beside himself with sorrow over his brother's feelings.

To have kept the film a straight drama would almost have been to shortchange the audience, with all of the great physical talent on the screen, though it would have made the film more popular with critics. When Hung and his friends play a game of cops and robbers in the street, they set off a series of incidents that build to the film's brutal finale. Hung unknowingly fools a mobster into thinking that he is a real cop, and the mobster drops a bag of cash. When the rest of the bad guys come to retrieve the money from him, Hung is made a suspect by the police, forcing Chan to act against his own beliefs as a cop and thwart police attempts to arrest Hung. After recovering the money, the mobsters kidnap Hung and want to exchange him for the mobster who lost the money in the first place. Any shred of sanity that Chan had shown earlier in the film is destroyed as he must forcibly rescue his brother. Chan recruits his SWAT team buddies for help, and they storm the building under construction that serves as a modern-day lair for these truly unsavory bad guys.

Heart of Dragon contains many familiar faces from the Hong Kong martial arts film world. Chan's SWAT team friends are played by Peking Opera brothers Yuen Kwai and Yuen Wah, stuntman Meng Hoi, and Hung protégé Chin Kar-lok. With bizarre-looking eyebrows, Lam Ching-ying plays the SWAT team commander. All of the bad guys are Hung regulars as well, most notably Dick Wei, Philip Ko Fei, and Chung Fat, who plays the mobster who lost the money. The best casting must be the mob boss, Chan's old Lo Wei bad guy James Tien. After the kung fu genre fizzled out, Hung used Tien in almost every film during the eighties. He played the mob boss in *Winners & Sinners* as well.

Heart of Dragon did well in Hong Kong, but the all-important Japanese market demanded an extra kick. Hung would go back and shoot two additional fight scenes: one in a hospital with Hung regular Lau Kar-wing and one in a parking lot, where Chan and his buddies fight off a group of kung fu heavies (including Fong Hak-on and Lee Hoi-san, Whang Inn-sik's villainous lackeys in *Young Master*). A Japanese cut of the film is the only version to include these two extra fight sequences, and it's worth the extra effort to track it down.

The acting of both Chan and Hung is top-notch, and no versions of the film do them justice except the Chinese and Japanese ones. In an interview with Hong Kong magazine *City Entertainment,* Chan pointed out that he doesn't do more dramatic roles because of this film. He said the drama worked quite well for Hong Kong audiences, but the international market just couldn't make any use of it.

There are three different soundtracks for the Chinese, Japanese, and British versions of the film. The music in the Chinese version is light, while the

Japanese version (by Kazuo Shiina) is somber and meaningful. This version also includes two Jackie Chan songs, "China Blue" and "Tokyo Saturday Night" (Chan sings the title in English). The latter, with a very catchy tune, is probably Chan's best song to date. The British-dubbed version includes happier-sounding music completely changing the tone of many of the scenes.

While none of the Chan features directed by Sammo Hung have out-takes at the end, the Japanese versions include these visual lessons of pain. *Heart of Dragon* contains the best out-take sequence of all of Hung's features. Although he is not in the film, Yuen Biao, who served as the film's martial arts instructor, appears briefly in the out-takes. The major highlight of the out-takes is an extremely dangerous fall that rivals Chan's drop from the clock tower in *Project A.* In the intended shot, Chung Fat is kicked through a window and falls off the second story, bouncing off an awning and landing on the top of a car. The out-take reel, however, shows stuntman Chung missing the awning altogether, falling straight to the ground—and if that wasn't bad enough, he gets hit by the car!

The last teaming up of Chan, Hung, and Yuen Biao came in *Dragons Forever.* It's clearly

Left to right: Yuen Wah, Chin Kar-lok, Meng Hoi, Jackie Chan, and Chan Lung. (*Colin Geddes/Asian Eye. By permission of Media Asia Group. © STAR TV*)

Dragons Forever (1988). (*Colin Geddes/Asian Eye. By permission of Media Asia Group. © STAR TV*)

one of Chan's most popular films (despite the fact that Chan's dressier wardrobe didn't suit the all-important Japanese audience). The film fuses together a nice mix of humor, eccentric characters, and more fighting than in any of Chan's other films. There is never a dull moment. Chan plays a womanizing defense lawyer who falls in love, fights his friends, and follows his instincts to a drug lord's hideout, where Hung is held hostage. When shooting was almost done, Benny Urquidez was once again contacted to fight Chan in the finale, while Yuen Biao and Sammo Hung fight off the usual crew. (For more on *Dragons Forever,* see chapter eleven, "Jackie's Sensational Seven.")

Jackie Chan will always be a singular star, and his work with Hung and Yuen Biao was revered as a classic teaming of talent. Unfortunately, it had to come to an end because Chan was bigger than the three combined. By the time *Project A* was released, Chan had already established his solo career as an international icon with his breakthrough kung fu comedies, something that Hung and Yuen couldn't have done on their own. *Police Story* set the precedent as Chan's greatest solo achievement, and he polished his filmmaking, choreography, editing, and acting skills, giving him the incentive to continue on his own. The more brutal action of *Police Story* shows Hung's influ-

ence, but Chan clearly had his own style.

Longtime Golden Harvest marketing officer Russell Cawthorne notes that "Yuen was more of the performer, while Sammo was more of the director. As for Jackie, he was a little bit of both." In exposing his two brothers to the international market, Chan enabled them to enjoy long careers in starring roles for several years after the three had split up.

What caused the three to break up? It's generally accepted that Hung was upset that Chan did not appear in Hung's epic *Shanghai Express* (also known as *Millionaire's Express,* 1987), which starred him and Yuen. Also, Yuen felt that Chan was getting more of the spotlight, so he wanted to venture out on his own as well. The result for Chan was bigger and better things. The result for Hung and Yuen was a kiss of death at the box office.

Hong Kong newspaper art. (*Colin Geddes/Asian Eye. By permission of Media Asia Group. © STAR TV*)

Hung, a flawed genius, takes incredible risks, both in style and in content, as an experimental filmmaker. Hung can easily be called the best action director the world has ever seen. In terms of content, however, Hung has shamelessly used sexism, racism, and other forms of bigotry to alienate his audiences from the Sammo Hung of the late seventies and early eighties. Hung even alienated Chan, causing a break in their friendship for a short time, rumored to be caused by Hung's excessive gambling problems. Golden Harvest gave Hung two opportunities to make the same type of big-budget films that Chan would lay claim to. Both *Shanghai Express* and *Eastern Condors* (1987) did poorly at the box office, however, and Hung's dip into the cookie jar for more money cast a dark shadow on his producing abilities. Hung left Golden Harvest in 1992 with *Moon Warriors*. On his own, Hung was able to direct and star in many films, using his own company, Bojon, to secure distribution. Most notably, *Pantyhose Hero* (1989), *Pedicab Driver* (1990), and the dark comedy *Slickers vs. Killers* (1992) show Hung's diversity in acting and stylish direction.

Falling heavily into debt, Hung eventually emigrated to America for a year and took up horse breeding to get his mind off things. Picking himself up off the ground, Hung returned to Hong Kong and in 1994 came back to the cinema. At the 1994 Hong Kong Film Awards, Chan, Hung, Yuen Biao, and several of their Peking Opera brothers presented an award. Hung was nominated for best fight choreography for the art film *Ashes of Time,* though he would lose to Chan and Lau Kar-leung's action in *Drunken Master II.* Hung then teamed back up with Yuen Biao for *Don't Give a Damn,* made as a favor to two of his sons, Hung Tin-ming and Hung Tin-cheung. Hung Tin-cheung has already started to follow his father's footsteps as a stuntman, breaking his nose shooting a commercial in 1996. (By the way, Jackie Chan is Hung Tin-ming's godfather and Yuen Woo-ping is Hung Tin-cheung's godfather.)

On July 7, 1995, Hung married his longtime girlfriend, Joyce "Mina" Godenzi, a femme fatale star Hung used in several action films like *Eastern Condors* and *She Shoots Straight.* When production of *Thunderbolt* ran into deadline problems, Golden Harvest asked Hung to choreograph the film's action scenes. It was the first collaboration between Hung and Chan since the lukewarm *Island of Fire* in 1991. With Hung's expert handling of the action, Chan was able to secure him as director of *Police Story V,* set in Sydney, Australia. Within a month the film title changed to *Mr. Nice Guy* and the setting to Melbourne, Australia. Sammo Hung was back in a major way, with a budget of over $25 million. Hung also returned to straight acting in *Somebody Up There Likes Me* (1995) and *Ah Kam* (1996), starring Michelle Yeoh. To bring things full circle, Hung teamed up with his old crew for *How to Meet the Lucky Stars* (1996). Jackie Chan and a number of industry heavies suggested the idea for this Lucky Stars film as a benefit for the near-bankrupt Lo Wei—all the film's principals worked for free. Unfortunately, Lo Wei died midway through shooting, the eventual proceeds went to his widow.

An entire book could be written about Sammo Hung's important contributions to the Hong Kong cinematic world, where the many notable directors and actors he has nurtured call him Big Brother in an echo of his Peking Opera school days. Hung has had a rough time in his comeback, but the world will finally see in 1997 what he learned from his time off. Not only will he have the director credit on *Mr. Nice Guy,* Chan's biggest action film to date, but he will have also directed the sixth installment of the popular Hwang Fei-hung series, *Once Upon A Time in China,* which was filmed in Brackettville, Texas. With both of these films opening during Chinese New Year 1997, Hung can't lose, no matter which film does better at the box office.

Yuen Biao's career has been just as flighty as the fantasy characters he often plays. Like Hung, Yuen was given a large sum for his directorial debut in *A Kid from Tibet* (1991), where Chan makes a brief cameo, but the film didn't perform to Golden Harvest's expectations. Yuen left Golden Harvest in 1992 (the same year as Hung) with *Shogun in Little Kitchen.* After leav-

Chan and Hung on the set of *Mr. Nice Guy* (1997). (*Courtesy of Golden Harvest*)

ing the company that had earned him so much fame abroad, Yuen would appear in multitudes of low-budget fantasy and action films over the next few years. Sinking to the very bottom, Yuen even started making Filipino-produced films, which is as low as one can go in Hong Kong filmmaking. The once-great actor, admired for his amazing acrobatic talents, seemed to be out of luck with no where to go.

Fortunately, in 1996 Yuen was able to land a strong lead in an as-yet-untitled gigantic fantasy film shot in mainland China over the course of a year. Directed by his Peking Opera brother Corey Yuen Kwai (who directed him in the high-octane action film *Righting Wrongs*, or *Above the Law*), this film could help Yuen Biao regain his old status within the Hong Kong cinema community.

Away from Jackie Chan, Yuen Biao's best films are *On the Run* (1988), a nonfighting police thriller; *The Champions* (1983), a soccer-kung fu film; *Iceman Cometh* (1989), a Chinese version of *Highlander*; and *The Prodigal Son*, which Sammo Hung directed. All of these were Golden Harvest productions.

For fans who have seen all of Jackie Chan's films, Sammo Hung and Yuen Biao appear in a plethora of their own interesting vehicles, which serve as worthy complements to Chan's work. They are more personalized, some have more action than others, and some even fall outside of the mainstream altogether, but one can't go too wrong renting one of Hung's or Yuen's films from the eighties.

Chan has summed up the trio's recent relationship in an interview during his *Rumble in the Bronx* US tour: [Sammo Hung] "is always the best. Now with Asia, everyone knows that Sammo is going down, and no one wants to see him in movies anymore. It's a very sad thing, so I called him up and we made a movie *[Mr. Nice Guy]* together again. So, right now Sammo can only direct; he cannot act. The film business is very bad. When you are a success, the film buyer is like, 'Oh, Sammo Hung—we want you, we need you.' But now the same buyer tells me, 'Please don't let Sammo direct or act in the movie.' It's very difficult. So now, I say, 'No, I clock tower fall in *Project A*, he did it not only once or twice but three times. The stunt is so amazing that he puts on film all three of his attempts back to back. Chan does the same thing with his fall in *Police Story*, as well as stunts in all of his modern films. It is common for a filmmaker to repeat a clip of a particularly interesting move, but when Chan shows a different angle or another attempt entirely, he is breaking the temporal plane in which the action rests. In a sense Chan is creating his own documents to his physical abilities.

In all of his directed features, Chan uses the scope format (aspect ratio 2.35:1), but not just because of his filmmaker's preference. The Shaw Brothers used this format (dubbed "Shaw Scope") for their kung fu films in the late sixties and seventies. This format gives the audience a complete view of the actor performing—there's little room for the director or anyone else to cheat. When Chan took the helm, he learned to command the wide screen as masterfully as Sergio Leone did with his "Man with No Name" spaghetti westerns. Chan has a knack for filling up the screen with action on the far left, the far right, and the middle simultaneously. Three of Chan's best films—both *Project A*'s and *Mr. Canton and Lady Rose*—almost look like substandard efforts if they are not shown in the correct aspect ratio. This aspect ratio can be seen on home videotape only in the letterbox format, where the horizontal is two and a half times as long as the vertical, the excess screen being blacked out. With wide-screen–angle lenses, another component of Keaton's filmmaking, it's difficult for Chan to cheat by exaggerating his physical abilities since all of the room around him is completely exposed. Tight shots are used only for basic dialogue sequences, while the majority of the action is kept in wide angles with the camera completely still. The intensity of the scene rests on the actors' abilities and not necessarily the editing.

The final element that makes all of Chan's films unique is his personal singing of the theme songs at either the beginning or the end. Like the bard who poetically chants of his amazing travels, Chan's theme songs are melodic leitmotifs of being that "unsung" hero. If he isn't going to sing about heroes, he sings about love in his ballads. Chan can sing in Cantonese and Mandarin, actually preferring the latter because he likes the flow of the language. (See the lyrics below.)

An interesting departure from his normal hero theme is in *Drunken Master II*. Here he relishes his drinking abilities, but the song is meant in good fun. After all, the film is a comedy, and he surely isn't trying to give kids the wrong idea about alcohol. The original theme song for Hwang Fei-hung in the now-famous *Once Upon a Time in China* series takes a different approach to the character—making him valiant and stoic. Coincidentally, Chan sung the second film's theme. Below is the first stanza from Hwang's more valiant portrayal from that series, followed by Chan's take.

Chan's most popular theme—the one in *Police Story*, used in parts one, two, and four (*First Strike*)—is followed by the theme for

Armour of God's murderous monks had little to do with religion. Here, Chan and his buddy Alan Tam try to infiltrate their ranks. (*Colin Geddes/Asian Eye. By permission of Media Asia Group. © STAR TV*)

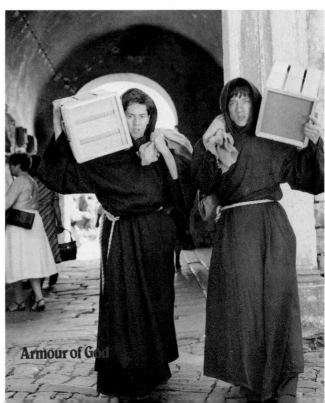

Armour of God

The Out-takes

The out-takes that run during the end credits of a Jackie Chan film have taken a life of their own—and they are another way he documents his physical abilities. Certainly they are one part of his films that everyone talks about, and it's easy to see why. Chan included random shots during the credits of *Young Master*, but after his experience with Hal Needham and the *Cannonball Run* films, the nature of the out-takes changed. Needham would always have a running credit reel (even extending past the credits) to show off Burt Reynolds and company's botched oneliners. While Needham and Chan never discussed the use of out-takes, it's clear that Chan sensed the crowd's enjoyment in watching them. For *Dragon Lord*'s end credits, Chan inserted scenes from the film with shots of mishaps on the set. By the time *Project A* came around, he could cover the entire credit sequence with nothing but out-takes. Chan's audiences let loose a continuous stream of "ooh"s and "aah"s as Chan is pummeled shot after shot. Now the audience expects to see this show of resilience and courage. Chan takes it all in good fun—singing in the background almost as if he were a wartorn soldier recounting his battle wounds. And that's exactly what they are.

Chan wants the audience to see his anguish, his blood, his labors—because he is doing all of this for them. During the credit reel for *Armour of God*, ambulance sirens replace the theme song as the accident that nearly cost him his life unreels. In *Drunken Master II*, when Chan leaps up after having his bottom raked across the coals, the audience can see the pain and agony as he wipes his face with a wet towel. His costars fare much the same: in *Police Story II* Maggie Cheung gets the top of her scalp ripped off from a falling metal frame. For the Japanese market, even Chan's collaborations with Sammo Hung are given these amazing credit reels as testaments of his willingness to please the audience at any cost. As Chan's films get more and more overblown in magnitude, the audience eagerly waits for the next dangerous display of real-life action. Never leave a Jackie Chan movie until all of the credits have appeared or, better yet, until the screen goes black.

Thunderbolt, although his hero in that film was a little more rigid than usual. This is a rare opportunity to see what Chan is actually singing about, because the songs are usually not translated on film for his non-Asian audiences.

.

"Once Upon a Time in China Theme" (first stanza only)

Facing the challenge with great confidence, I see
    blood spraying like the red sunshine.
I am fearless, courageous. I got the body of steel.
I do what no one can do, and I see what no one
    can see.
I fight for my life, I struggle to be a man.
To be a man, you got to be stronger day by day.

"Drunken Master II Theme"
I'm bumping up and down, seems like I would
    fall.

Laughing is my answer toward all the pain and
    sadness.
I go low and I go high.
I am swaying back and forth, but I never fall,
because I know all there is to know about the art
    of drinking.

Fighting for fame, I never use a blade.
Carrying all the weight on my own shoulders.
I never beg and never plead, to anyone or any-
    thing.
But I don't mind giving in to passion and
    honor,
As the god of drunkenness, I'm a great man.

Don't call me crazy, 'cause a crazy man like me
    has a warm heart.
Don't call at me silly, 'cause silly man with a
    loyal heart is hard to find.
Don't be afraid of drunkenness, drunken as I am

Chan, underdressed in the Ukraine and with alarming head gear, proves he's no James Bond in *First Strike*. (*Courtesy of Golden Harvest*)

Tong uses his new locales and other devices to highlight cultural differences. When Chan becomes lost, not even having his bearings (another defused Bondism), he must read a Russian sign to his CIA contact and a translator

Chan inspects the lion prior to the funeral sequence. (*Courtesy of Golden Harvest*)

on a mobile phone. He gets a puzzled look on his face and finally blurts out, "Backwards N?!" which only the Russian translator understands. When Uncle Seven, Tsui's mafia boss father, is killed, Chan tries to convince his superiors that Low will be at the funeral. Chan's superiors challenge him on this, and he explains that it is a ceremonial duty for the only son of the deceased to carry out the funeral traditions. There is even a reference to differing Chinese beliefs with the funeral sequence in general. White is the symbolic color of death, the one most often associated with funerals in Chinese culture, yet the scene in *First Strike* is in black and white. Tong explains, "The reason why we put black with the hearses is because the character in the scene . . . has lived there [Australia] for so many years—it's a mixed culture. Australian-Chinese is very different from Hong Kong Chinese." Several times during the film, Chan even has to ask the other Chinese players to speak in Mandarin instead of English.

Stanley Tong's storyboard for a sequence never shot. (*Courtesy of Stanley Tong and Golden Harvest*)

Even a difficult stunt was storyboarded for Tong's brand of action. (*Courtesy of Stanley Tong and Golden Harvest*)

Once again Tong uses a great deal of light humor to break the dryness of the story. From Chan wearing koala bear underwear to sucking on a bloody thumb to avoid a shark attack, *First Strike* is appealing to those who like something cute or humorous to balance out the more masculine antics of spies, international espionage, and good, old-fashioned action sequences. As for the action itself, the film changes the whole shooting match on the audience for the third time. *Supercop* was all Tong, *Rumble* was more Chan, and *First Strike* is almost all Tong, except for one of Chan's classic prop fights.

When this film was released, hardly anyone noted its story, acting, and settings as benefits. The action—or lack of it—was the main topic of concern about *First Strike*, and Chan's fans weren't satisfied. Tong's defense is that "Jackie has already done so many different types of action sequences and has fought for so many years, that it's hard to find something that has never been done before. We had to come up with something like this to compete with the big-budgeted American pictures." Tong is correct in the sense that Chan has fought so many times on screen that it would literally be impossible for him to throw some new kind of punch or kick. His theory also translates into bringing realism to the film where exhaustive kung fu sequences would look implausible.

The film does have complete diversity of action, from the large-scale ski battle to the funeral gunfight, from Chan's tangle with ladders to the underwater finale with sharks and armed scuba divers. The amazing ski attack, a lavish display of Tong's masterful use of the widescreen, showed off the beautiful scenery of Falls Creek, Australia. The sequence was shot over the course of twenty-five days, and Chan received only four days of training for the snowboard.

Tong adhered to his complex storyboards for filming the sequence but ended up cutting two of the scene's potential gags. The more complex one sends Chan flying over the top of a tall pine, so that he grabs the top of the tree as he passes over it. Pulling the top back like cocking a spring, he lets it go, hitting the unsuspecting bad guy skier in the face. According to the storyboards, it would have been an amazing shot if it had made it into the final cut. In the other excised sequence, inspired by a similar gag in *The Spy Who Loved Me*, Chan was next going to topple down a three-story-house's rooftop with several skiers right behind him. Since helicopters were dropping these skiers right overhead, the gag would have had one of them fall directly into the chimney. Upon landing on the ground, in another fantastic one-shot, two skiers would come racing right over Chan's head!

The ski sequence that does make the final cut is exhilarating, building up to a climax that sends Chan jumping off of the mountain onto a helicopter, only to have his cap clipped off by the helicopter blades! Before the helicopter is blown up by the attackers' helicopter, Chan falls into an ice-covered lake, breaking through the ice into the freezing water. Although Tong did the fall from the helicopter, Chan was the one who nearly got hypothermia by staying in the water too long wearing next to nothing.

After the comical chase scene of running away from the giant Russian, Chan directs the trademark Jackie Chan fight scene inside of an Australian museum. Without storyboards, it was back to the improvisational style for which Hong Kong fight scenes are known. It took fourteen days to film the seven-minute scene, and ranged from hand to hand to poles to dragon heads to ladders. Though it ranks as another classic fight montage, something was missing. Chan fights throughout the entire scene completely in defense. He does not engage the enemy but merely reacts. This is perhaps the one flaw to Tong's take on Chan's action. Usually, Chan reacts until he can't take any more, and then he turns into the aggressor. At no point does this happen in *First Strike*.

First Strike's detailed plotline brought Chan out of his world and into a more realistic setting. There is no denying the restraint of Chan's *First Strike* character, but the film tries to stay as realistic as possible. Since Chan's own genre of filmmaking exists in a microcosm of pseudo-reality where implausibility reigns, it's only fair to let Tong keep *that* character at bay. *First Strike*

Real ice.

Real cold. (*Courtesy of Golden Harvest*)

is the first Chan film to try to stay story-driven instead of letting the character run amuck. Even *Supercop* had its own brand of zaniness to exploit its humor as well as its characters.

Yet the realism breaks down: The film's finale is the most unrealistic sequence in any of Chan's films. The twenty-minute underwater battle has Chan and Tsui's sister (Chien Chun-wu) trying to retrieve the U-235, while the bad guys do the same. The extra obstacles are that Chan doesn't have an oxygen tank and there are man-eating sharks in the aquarium tank with them. There are some great moments, but the sequence drags on far too long, and some critics found it ridiculous. Tong defends the finale:

"Everyone in Asia likes that scene. I don't think any other action star could get away with it, but for Jackie Chan, it's okay to have him do silly things."

Originally, underwater specialist Ron Taylor of *Jaws* fame was to aid in shooting the climax, but Tong had to take over since Taylor had no experience shooting an action sequence of this magnitude. Tong spent nearly a million dollars in constructing a tank for the film, but it kept leaking every day. Finally, Tong moved to shooting in a real aquarium, but the set had to be dismantled during business hours for tourists. Tong also built three mechanical sharks, though he says that most of the shark footage in the film was of the real thing. A shot of a diver's leg hanging out of a shark's mouth, however, is part of the silliness that undermines the realism Tong was trying to bring to the film.

In the end *First Strike* looks like a $40-million Hollywood film with real action. Even the rockets fired from helicopters were on wires, with just a touch of animation to conceal the obvious. No computer effects or miniatures—everything was done right there. Unsurprisingly, postproduction lasted only ten days after principal photography. If this film had been done in America, CGI effects would have replaced the mechanical sharks and most of the stunt work, putting postproduction time into months instead of days. No joke.

Tong doesn't consider himself a Hong Kong filmmaker but an international filmmaker: "I was always told that if I wanted to make an American film, I would have to go to America, but it would not work in Asia. And vice versa. I don't believe it. If you shoot something Hong Kong style, you will show favor to Asian tastes. If you shoot something international style, you will favor international tastes." Tong is an honest, hard-working filmmaker who is still young enough to have dreams of making his kind of movies, not Hollywood's longer music videos.

Having signed with Ruddy Morgan and Associates to represent him, Tong was immediately inundated with projects from many differ-

Ad for *To Kill with Intrigue*. (*Colin Geddes/Asian Eye*)

Chan fights Kam Kong in *Half a Loaf of Kung Fu*. (*Colin Geddes/Asian Eye*)

Drunken Master. (*Colin Geddes/Asian Eye*)

The Three Kung-fu-teers: Sammo Hung, Yuen Biao, and Chan in *Dragons Forever*. (Media Asia Group. © STAR TV)

Supercop. (By permission of Media Asia Group. © STAR TV)

City Hunter. (Colin Geddes/Asian Eye. By permission of Media Asia Group. © STAR TV)

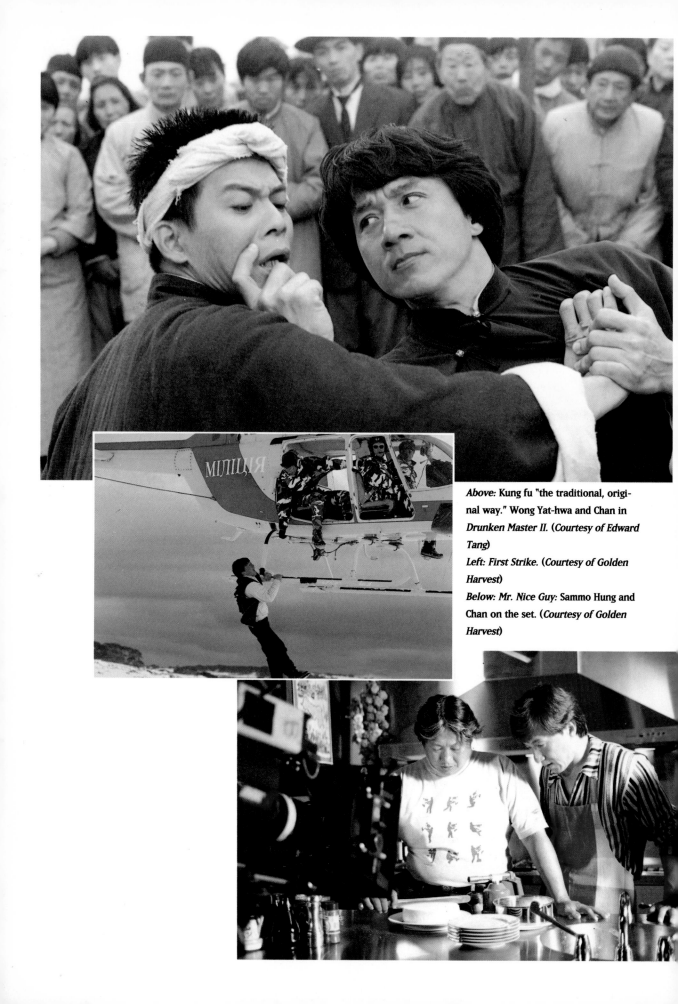

Above: Kung fu "the traditional, original way." Wong Yat-hwa and Chan in *Drunken Master II.* (*Courtesy of Edward Tang*)
Left: First Strike. (*Courtesy of Golden Harvest*)
Below: Mr. Nice Guy: Sammo Hung and Chan on the set. (*Courtesy of Golden Harvest*)

ent film companies. Tong's American debut will not be a typical action film at all, but a live-action version of the popular cartoon "Mr. Magoo," starring Leslie Nielson. Tong's real test will be an expensive international film entitled *Wet Works*, described by Tong as a "reinvention of *Charlie's Angels* meets *Mission: Impossible*." Scripted by Tong, the film will star one Chinese woman (popular Hong Kong actress Christy Chung), one African-American woman (Halle Berry), and one Hispanic-American woman (Salma Hayek). They are in for a ride since Tong plans on having this trio perform their own stunts.

With Tong's bright outlook, anything is possible. However, the Chinese part of Tong will not be diminished even if he is making a Hollywood film: "I was born and raised in Hong Kong, so I don't think I could make as good of a straight American film as an American director. I still have many stories to tell about Chinese culture, so I want to try and combine the two until I can learn more about American culture." Part of that culture, in terms of the cinema, is

Stanley Tong directs *First Strike*'s **funeral sequence.**
(*Courtesy of Golden Harvest*)

using that eight- to twelve-week shooting schedule to work in the inventive action sequences for which Hong Kong directors are known. One only hopes he will have more luck in America than John Woo, whose style has been watered down in paint-by-number buddy pictures.

Jackie's Other Children

Sammo Hung and Stanley Tong are the only two directors who could do what Chan wanted them to do in the first place. They both commanded their film sets with firm authority—taking the pressure off Chan, whose mind was left to rest on acting and action. Tong brought structure and attention to his work, and Chan respected his drive as well as the amazing personal similarities between the two. Hung's experience spanned the course of nearly two hundred films, with jobs as producer, actor, fight choreographer, and director. "Jackie never once challenged Sammo's direction. I remember asking Yuen Biao if he ever second-guessed him. He said, 'No one does. Not even Jackie. Jackie is my big brother; Sammo is everyone's big brother. Nobody questions big brother!'" says *Wheels on Meals* vet Keith Vitali.

As long as Chan could see that the director was in control at all times, there was no need for intervention. Control is a factor of Chan's filmmaking, and that is the key to using him instead of being used by him. Directors Tsui Hark, Wong Jing, Kirk Wong, Lau Kar-leung, and Gordon Chan were put to the test. All of them failed for one reason or another.

Twin Dragons and Double Impact

As a charity effort for the Hong Kong Film Director's Guild, *Twin Dragons* (1992) was a comedic fluff piece, with Chan's amiable charm showing through with not one but two characters. Born to a prominent family, two

City Hunter. (Colin Geddes/Asian Eye. By permission of Media Asia Group. © STAR TV)

Twin Dragons. (Colin Geddes/Asian Eye. By permission of Media Asia Group. © STAR TV))

who has managed to land himself in quite a mess with a group of unruly mobsters. Both Chans are connected to women (Maggie Cheung and Nina Li-chi) that are better suited for each other's twin, leading to the endless mistaken-identity gags that form most of the film's humor. After the two twins reunite, they make a pact to get the mechanic Chan out of trouble and deal with their lady friends accordingly.

After an incredible display of Chan's kicking power in the beginning, the film's action settles down to a more restrained level until the climactic showdown in a car testing center, where Chan's team takes over to full effect. Chan rips through assorted props that one would find in such a place, and he must fight Shaw Brothers veteran villain Wang Lung-wei *(Project A II).*

In all fairness, the film is cute, and some of the one-note humor's scenarios are slightly amusing. There is the obvious fantasy element of seeing two Chans on the screen at once, and the whole film was made with good, clean fun in mind. Whenever one Chan does something, the other feels it and reacts to it. This part of the gag quickly loses its novelty, but *Twin Dragons* was a limited idea in the first place. At least the film does make good use of this device when the nonfighting Chan must use his twin to throw his punches for him.

Part of the reason that Chan wanted to do this film was to experiment with special effects, using the master Hong Kong director of such, Tsui Hark. "Compared to Hollywood special effects, *Twin Dragons* is crap!" states Chan. "After that, I'm totally disappointed with Hong Kong special effects. This is why I'm not going

twins are separated at the hospital by a crazed killer on the loose. One twin ends up with a town drunk and grows up to be an auto mechanic, complete with ponytail, earring, and smoking habit. The other twin grows up with his family in America and becomes a praised composer and pianist. The *Prince and the Pauper* retelling soon comes into full swing when composer Chan comes to Hong Kong for his first big concert away from home. There he runs into the mechanic, also played by Chan, to use special effects in my films again, except from the people in Hollywood." Surprisingly, though, most of the effects featuring both Chans on the screen at the same time are comparable to some of Hollywood's bigger-budgeted efforts, like *Big Business* (1988).

Twin Dragons directors Tsui Hark and Ringo Lam have both turned out some of the greatest Hong Kong films on their own. Tsui's films are politically charged poems of Chinese enlightenment, while Lam stays close to hard-edged police dramas set in murky urban locales. Together they trade in their personal styles for that of the loosely structured comedies they made at the start of their careers—both of them directed sequels in the *Aces Go Places* series. Sadly, neither director's vision really shows through, and the only highlights are the action sequences and occasional charm by Chan and company.

Twin Dragons was also a reunion of sorts, since Ng See-yuen served as producer and Yuen Woo-ping assisted in the film's fight choreography. More than fifty Hong Kong directors made cameos in the film, including Wong Jing *(City Hunter)* as a supernatural healer, Lau Kar-leung *(Drunken Master II)* as a doctor, Kirk Wong *(Crime Story)* as the crazed killer and John Woo *(Hand of Death)* as a priest. When Chan first enters the car testing center, the three guys sitting at a table playing cards are Tsui Hark, Ringo Lam, and Ng See-yuen. *Twin Dragons* was

Chan in action. (*Colin Geddes/Asian Eye. By permission of Media Asia Group. © STAR TV*))

inspired by the Jean-Claude Van Damme film *Double Impact*. (Van Damme has made a film each with Ringo Lam, *Maximum Risk*, and Tsui Hark, *Double Team*.)

City Hunter and the Prolific Wong Jing

Due to *Supercop*'s marginal success, Golden Harvest urged Chan to keep costs down and make a couple of smaller films. *City Hunter* and *Crime Story* could not be any further apart in tone, action, and direction. Based on the *manga* (comic book) and associated animation series, *City Hunter* (1992) seemed like the perfect vehicle with the Japanese market in mind. Chan's character, Ryu Saeba, is a womanizing detective whose nifty theme music appears whenever he does anything. Chan's films stretch the notion of plausibility, but *City Hunter* allowed him to go into pure escapism. "We wanted Wong Jing to direct *City Hunter* because he is real good at keeping costs down and knows how to control budgets. Besides, he knows how to direct comic book movies," says Chua Lam, *City Hunter*'s producer. Wong is Hong Kong's Roger Corman, a low-budget, prolific purveyor of madness. If Wong's name appears in the credits, the audience should know better than to look for continuity or balance. Even with his scattershot efforts, Wong has managed to direct some win-

Maggie Cheung and Chan. (*Colin Geddes/Asian Eye. By permission of Media Asia Group. © STAR TV*))

Chan and Daniels, in *Streetfighter II* wardrobe, stop for a quick pose. (*Courtesy of Gary Daniels*)

fight with Kareem Abdul-Jabbar to get the upper hand with his towering opponents. Jackie Chan has worked hard to stay away from the stereotype of being just another Bruce Lee clone, but it was nice to see that he could take a tip from the Little Dragon when need be.

Chan's other concern is playing for the affections of Joey Wang, which leads to a fight with Gary Daniels when she tries to make Chan

Chan's first meeting with Gary Daniels. (*Courtesy of Gary Daniels*)

jealous. The duel is fairly noteworthy and comical, but Chan was supposed to be the one to shine, so Daniels wasn't given the chance to display any of his own acrobatic abilities. After Daniels had left, Kenneth Low was inserted for an overhead shot without Daniels's knowledge. If one looks closely, one can clearly see Low's face under a long blonde wig. That blonde hair of Daniels was precisely what landed him the job in *City Hunter* anyway, since the best gag in the film is a dreamlike sequence where the characters from the Streetfighter II arcade game come to life. Daniels is a mirror image of the game's Ken, two Hong Kong disc jockeys known as the Hard and Soft Team played Guile and Dhalsim, and Chan himself played E. Honda and Chun Li. The movements and sound effects emulate the game with complete accuracy, something that the American *Streetfighter*, starring Jean-Claude Van Damme, did not.

In *Half a Loaf of Kung Fu*, Chan uses his female costar as a prop, flipping her around his body while she throws kicks and punches at the enemy. Fifteen years later Chan uses Chingmy Yau (an agent assigned to the ship) in a similar fashion, only this time she is shooting all of the guns fastened to different parts of her body. When a Taiwanese commando unit comes to the rescue, the only thing left is a climactic battle with Richard Norton, shot on the Shaw Brothers lot. Using conventional means, Norton assails Chan with fists and feet, sticks, and, finally, whips. Chan, on the other hand, breakdances around Norton's actions, even executing a gymnastic iron cross move when given the chance. Although Chan did this particular move himself, some of the action was doubled by a Mainland Chinese gymnast. Again, these days when Chan doesn't have the time to prepare himself for his stunts and have his crew around him for support, doubles will be used more readily. In shooting two films back to back,

Three years later, Wong Jing would end up directing a parody of Jackie Chan himself in *High Risk*. Hong Kong pop star Jacky Cheung plays a pretentious action star whose fame and fortune have diminished his will to perform his own stunts. Jet Li plays the character that stunt-doubles for him, though Li was doubled in the scenes he was supposed to be doing for real. Jacky Cheung's manager in the film is the spitting image of Willie Chan, though all of the characters in the film are played so silly that any harmful statement regarding Jackie Chan's stunt-doubling was surely unintended.

"Jackie would show up around one o'clock in the afternoon, do a shot, and then fall asleep, before he had to go to the other set at night," remembers Daniels.

Crime Story and the Darker Shades of Kirk Wong

Imagine bringing the cold hardships of the real world to Chan's *Police Story* character and you've got *Crime Story* (1993). Instead of running around in a loose shirt and slacks, Chan has the stuffiness of a detective bound in a tie, pressed pants, and jacket. He doesn't kung fu everyone into submission, either, because his world uses guns to proclaim authority. Even his typical "man versus himself" conflict reveals a darker side here. He has to see a police psychologist on a regular basis to keep his sensibilities despite the anxieties that plague his day-to-day work. All of these great character traits would have made for an interesting departure from the Jackie Chan genre, but forty minutes into it, the only thing that remained was the blue-tinted look of the film.

In 1991 when Chan was filming *Twin Dragons,* one of the easiest directors to cast as an actor was Kirk Wong Chi-keung as the film's villain, a role that he played countless times during the eighties. Wong's directing career was on shaky ground at the time, and he had this idea of bringing a true crime story from 1990 to the screen. In discussing the idea, Chan liked the story very much, but Wong had Mainland Chinese kung fu star Jet Li in mind for the role. When Li left Golden Harvest after a falling out with director Tsui Hark, Wong's script was dead in the water. Thinking it over, Chan expressed interest in taking the lead because he was curious about the film's background and wanted another shot at a straight acting job.

What Chan didn't understand was Kirk Wong's style. In 1981 Wong unleashed *The Club*, an exploitive gangland thriller using kung fu star and ex-triad member Chan Hui-man in the lead role. From this directorial debut, it was apparent that Wong's vision revealed the darker side of protagonists caught up in personal conflict. Moods are set by exposing the underbelly of the modernized world, where neon lights dance across the smoke-filled sky. Much of the sound used in his films stems from the hustle and bustle of normal city life such as the vibrations of a jackhammer, the clamor of a crowded street, and the crackling pops of food being fried by local vendors.

Violence is not abundant, but the emotions that drive what is on the screen is even more heart-pounding, if not entirely conceivable. In *Gunmen* (1988) a child blows away the lead villain with a blood-spouting head shot. In *Rock n' Roll Cop* (1993) a man splatters a cat against a wall with his bare hands. In *Health Warning* (1984) a man is stabbed in the back with rabies-infected syringes. If Chan had fully understood Kirk Wong's films, he probably would not have appeared in *Crime Story* at all, much less modify the film to suit his own needs.

The film is based on the 1990 kidnapping of a high-profile land developer who had also been kidnapped just two years before. The land developer calls again for police aid, and Chan is assigned to the case. The kidnappers demand US$60 million for the developer's safe return, but Chan's team quickly figures out where the money is going. The only problem is that one of Chan's team, a decorated police officer he admires (played by veteran character actor Kent Cheng), turns out to be one of the culprits. When he and Chan follow a lead to Taiwan, Chan becomes suspicious of Cheng. Chan is forced to carry out his own personal investigation upon their return to Hong Kong. The plot shifts from the kidnapping itself to the cat and mouse game between Chan and Cheng.

Along with the changing of central plotlines, Chan apparently took the helm away from Wong. Though he didn't work on the film, Edward Tang has noted that Chan was not happy with the subplot involving his character's mental strain. Thus, after two scenes where Chan and the police psychologist bump heads, she is excised from the film altogether. An awkward relationship was supposed to have surfaced between the two, revealing even more of Chan's inner conflict, but this whole plot strain was completely done away with.[1] "Wong made the film look too serious with the blue and discolored lenses; Jackie just wanted to lighten things up," remembers Golden Harvest producer Chua Lam.

In the beginning of the film, Wong's trademark shooting style is left intact, with hand-held cameras, elaborate crane shots, and blue-tinted lenses. The violence is heavy hitting without being over the top. As for Wong's unrealistic, yet original violent exercises, there is a scene where the kidnappers must revive a woman with jumper cables while revving up the engine! Even Chan's head receives a bloodletting gash when his car rolls over.

When sex is used in Wong's films, it is often not as a show of love, but of aggression. There is a scene in the film where Cheng and his mistress grope each other in an elevator. This is followed by a heated scene in an underground parking lot. When Chan saw this, he snapped at Wong that this was not something that could appear in a Jackie Chan movie. In the release these seedy proceedings are faded out into the scene that follows.

Chan's character is at first afraid, hesitant, and shaken when drawn into violence. During a

shoot-out at the beginning of the film, Chan unloads his gun from behind a car, while a child is not more than three feet in the background. The sprays of gunfire lighting up the streets of Hong Kong preclude him from saving the child—only himself.

With the police psychologist subplot taken out, however, Chan suddenly becomes more physically courageous. Two scenes show the incredible contradiction between the sides of his character. First Chan goes to Cheng's mistress's club, where many of the kidnappers are there to greet him. They throw wine on him and push him around, and Kenneth Low gives him a nice, big smooch on the lips to agitate him. Chan merely walks away from the encounter without so much as a punch or a kick staying within the character the film originally portrays. Not fifteen minutes later, however, when he brings in one of the bad guys, they tear up police headquarters with normal Chan fare. After finishing him off, Chan does a forward somersault to land himself in front of a water fountain to quench his thirst. From there on, Kirk Wong's style and his control of the film is lost to Chan.

The film does have some great stunts, and although they are not as big as Chan's usual set pieces, they should keep fans happy. After the change in characters and action, the finale, thankfully, returns to Kirk Wong's style, although it bears more resemblance to Sammo Hung's *Heart of Dragon* climax. Chan's inability to save the kidnapping victim leads him to a dilapidated locale in Kowloon, where he tries to make sense out of a code associated with Cheng's part in the crime. Little does he know that he is standing in the kidnappers' lair and must face off against nearly ten men armed with guns, shovels, chairs, and anything else they could get their hands on. *Heart of Dragon*'s cinematographer, Arthur Wong, worked on this film to pull off some of the fantastic shots, particularly in this end sequence. Aside from Kenneth Low, Sammo Hung's kung fu man Chung Fat also makes an appearance as one of the kidnappers. Although Chan choreographed the film, he let his *Snake and Crane Arts of Shaolin* director Chen Chi-wah do all of the fight directing.

[1] The screenwriter must have been more upset than Wong: he was the real-life police officer that Chan was portraying.

Chen's style brings back more of the brutality, which complements Kirk Wong's vision.

After this amazing encounter, the entire building blows up due to a gas leak. Chan once again goes against his original characterization when one of Cheng's men is burning to death. Instead of trying to save him, Chan shoots him to death to end his misery. Then, in completely contradictory behavior, he tries to aid Cheng's escape from the building after Cheng had tried to trap Chan and a small child there to seal their fates!

For fans wishing to see what Wong should have done with Chan's character, check out *Rock 'n' Roll Cop,* where the protagonist walks attentively towards his enemy with a deathly stare. After a blistering fight, he leans the villain up against the wall and blows his head off. A word is never uttered during the entire confrontation. Wong's style may not necessarily suit America—nor Jackie Chan, for that matter—but it echoes the true nature of violence and the fevered pain that drives it. In Hollywood the good guy and the bad guy stand there and talk to each other for a few minutes before the bad guy gets shot in the arm. Then he gets up to attack again, forcing the good guy to finally kill him. Is this how it would really happen?

After *Crime Story* the Hong Kong film industry had its new genre to tap into: true crime. This genre produced dozens of films over the course of 1994. Wong released *Organized Crime and Triad Bureau* (one of the first Hong Kong films marketed to the non-Asian market during the nineties). With renewed interest in his gritty filmmaking style, Wong moved to America and presently resides in Los Angeles. He will be helming *The Big Hit*, an action comedy, for Wesley Snipes' new company.

Drunken Master II and Hwang Fei-Hung's Relative

In 1991, elitist New Wave director Tsui Hark made a daring move by bringing the kung fu film back to Hong Kong cinema with *Once Upon a Time in China.* Gone were the days of

(By permission of Media Asia Group. © STAR TV)

The most puzzling aspect of *Thunderbolt* is its use of three different directors. Gordon Chan had worked as a scriptwriter (he coscripted *Dragons Forever*) and effects supervisor before he became a director himself in 1989. Action was not his game, since he directed mostly dramas and comedies. For the majority of *Thunderbolt*, Gordon Chan was in charge of handling the dialogue. For the racing sequences Frankie Chan was brought in, due to his knowledge of racing. He had directed *The Outlaw Brothers* (1988), an even mix of car racing and martial arts fight scenes, which Jackie Chan assisted on as a favor. Although he was a director himself (he codirected *Armour of God II*), Frankie Chan was known more for being a composer, writing music for *Young Master* and *Winners & Sinners*. With Sammo Hung to direct the action sequences, it would seem that *Thunderbolt* would have a major flow problem. Shooting in Hong Kong, Japan, and Malaysia, producer Chua Lam coordinated all three directors and their various tasks. In the end, however, Gordon Chan's directing style completely lost out to the other talents involved. A similar occurrence happened with Gordon Chan's *Fist of Legend*, where action director Yuen Woo-ping virtually turned it into his movie.

Once the story was changed from its original conception, it became the dumbest plotline ever to be used in a Jackie Chan film. The corny story has to do with a murderous race car driver named Cougar who decides to go to Hong Kong to stir up trouble. While his original intentions are never revealed (a scene that supposedly takes place in Los Angeles gives the only clue to his crimes), this Aussie racer just burns rubber around the streets of Hong Kong, eventually catching the attention of the local police.

To assist them, the police hire a group of professional racing mechanics, one of them being Chan, to capture the speedster at his own game. When Chan traps him, Cougar vows to take revenge by racing him in Japan, noting his skills as a race car driver(?)! After Chan declines, Cougar tries to persuade him to race by fighting him at his garage, but this just leads to Chan lying to the police to seal Cougar's apprehension. After a bloody escape, Cougar and his men literally turn Chan's world upside down by lifting his home—a train car—with a crane and dropping it, injuring his father. Cougar's men then kidnap his sisters in the process. In secret, an infuriated Chan and his crew leave for Japan to race Cougar and save his sisters.

Rumble in the Bronx had its problems with bad guys without agendas, but *Thunderbolt*'s conflict was so ludicrous that even a straight-to-video movie would have more originality. Jackie Chan's character becomes the strong silent type, a humble working man who was once a great race car driver but just wants to be another mechanic working with his family. The film showed promise by bringing in Hong Kong star Anita Yuen as a roving reporter out to make Chan a local hero. She is curious about Chan's nature, and it looked like the two would fall for each other. Nothing really happens, though, except for the repeated lines of dialogue concerning his lack of interest in being interviewed.

Instead of Chan always being on the defensive, as in Tong's films, Chan becomes the aggressor in *Thunderbolt*, a key element to making Sammo Hung's two fight sequences even more gratifying. While an amazing fight sequence in a Japanese pachinko parlor reminds viewers of the good ol' days of *Dragons Forever*, the fifteen-minute car chase at the end of *Thunderbolt* was supposed to be the real action. As it turned out, it looks more like Hal Needham on acid; the scenes are so undercranked that the intensity and stuntwork look even more cartoonish than one of Chan's fight sequences. Chua Lam explains why this was done: "If you go to Japan to shoot, you'll know why things cost so much. After shooting there for a few weeks, there were so many injuries and costs ran so high that we had to move to Malaysia to finish the scene. In slowing down the cars, we could shoot everything just once, and then speed it up for the finished product." The finale does provide some great stunt work, especially a shot where a car crashes through a lookout tower, but the film is so sped up that it detracts from the serious effort put into the scene. Some of the footage had to have been shot at less than twenty frames per second compared to twenty four!

If one isn't expecting too much, at least *Thunderbolt* looks better than many of Chan's other films in terms of style, and there are some stunning visuals. In keeping with Tong's synch-sound efforts, the film was shot mostly in Cantonese, but at least 10% was shot in English and another 5% in Japanese. Sammo Hung's two fight sequences are mesmerizing to watch, although many viewers complained that his varied filmmaking techniques were too much on the eyes.

Due to Chan's injury in *Rumble in the Bronx* and the rushed production of the film, much of Chan's fight action was doubled out by Hung protégé Chin Kar-lok, who has been dubbed "Jackie Junior." Chin is an amazing stuntman, martial artist, and actor in his own right, most recently praised with a nomination for a film on motorcycle racing entitled *Full Throttle.* Though Hung can usually mask doubles fairly well, there were just too many behind shots giving the double away. Chan does pull off some of the stunts himself, but he was resting up for *First Strike,* where he used a double only a few times during the snowboard sequence.

Jackie Chan explains why control means so much to him and why he still gives the original director credit on the marquee: "Because I'm chairman of the Director's Guild, I can't say, 'You're out—Jackie Chan direct!' I think that's not fair. I still put their names in because you have to know the person, and many times I don't have time to know the director. For some directors, everything is just business. You sign the contract, you get the money. They don't care.

"I care about the movie. . . . When I go see the rushes and say, 'What the hell is that? Rubbish!' they just continue to do these types of things. If they get fired, it's okay. For me, I make movies for my audience and for myself." The reason for this is that aside from everything else, Chan wants each film to be just as special as the one before it. He does not believe in giving the audience only half of what a Jackie Chan film can be, just for the sake of making a quick buck.

Believe it or not, Chan has denounced all of the films discussed in this chapter, including *Drunken Master II* (although he shows some ambivalence). For obvious reasons, he absolutely hated *City Hunter, Twin Dragons,* and *Thunderbolt.* In watching these aborted children of his, one does get to see the range that Jackie Chan has as an actor. From excruciatingly goofy to somberly aggressive, however, these characters embody the traits unbefitting his own genre. Whether he will experiment even more with other Hong Kong directors remains a mystery, but these characterizations are duly noted as personas that weren't meant to be.

The Personal Side

After Chan had been in America for only a month shooting *The Big Brawl*, Wong Jiu-tu interviewed him for a Hong Kong English-language magazine called *Jacky Chan: His Privacy and Personal Anecdotes*. Chan was quoted as saying, "I wish I can fight my way into the international market.... For the movies I did for Golden Harvest, the dialogue, the plot, etc. have all been tailored to suit the foreign market. My only wish at present is that at least I want the foreign people to know that I'm Jackie Chan, and I've made a reputation for the Chinese." Chan's wish turned into an exhausting quest to entertain audiences worldwide—a quest that has consumed his personal life.

Jackie Chan is definitely one for trying to keep his personal life to himself and not the media. He takes on his "underdog character" as his true-life persona, even though he is surrounded by the glitz and glamour of stardom. Chan considers his close friends, his movies, and his fans his family.

Chan was secretly married in 1983 to Lin Feng-chiao (Lum Fang-gew), with whom he has one son, born the same year. Lin was one of the most famous actresses of the late sixties in Taiwan and Hong Kong. Often the careers of Chinese actresses are short because once they get married, they retire. Lin was at the peak of her career, but upon her marriage to Chan, she retired from the film industry. Chan was not ready for that kind of relationship, however. He has been separated from her for quite some time, though he stays in contact with her and their son. He has insured that they will be

Japanese ad celebrating Chan's ten years of directing and starring in his own films. (*Colin Geddes/Asian Eye*)

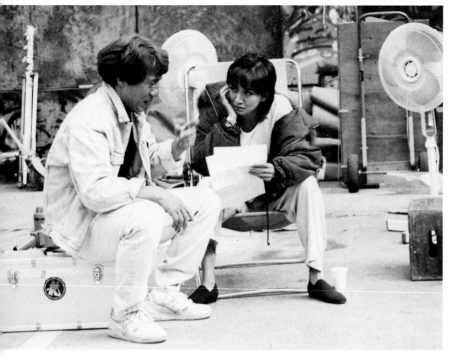

Chan and Anita Mui on the set of *Rumble in the Bronx.*
(*Courtesy of Edward Tang*)

But he's more than that—he's an international icon, appealing to many people from differing cultures with varying beliefs and ideals. In an effort to please the greatest number of people, he tries to keep quiet about his own beliefs—or is ambiguous. Chan even claimed that he doesn't believe in God or Buddha because religion has caused great turmoil and warfare for centuries, and that he wants nothing to do with it. Chan's personal convictions are exhibited through his films, which he has been quoted as calling his other children. With this thinking, it's no wonder that he takes such care with his films' growth/production.

In taking a cue from Bojon, a company Sammo Hung founded in 1980, Chan created his own film company, Golden Way, in 1984. The company gave him the chance to put his creativity behind the camera in many different ways. Instead of renting, Chan bought all of his own cameras, lighting, and gaffing equipment for his films. Like Hung, he saw the need to produce

financially secure for the rest of their lives, and Lin oversees several of the homes Chan owns in Taiwan.

Chan does have girlfriends, but relationships with this world-famous movie star are difficult. The Japanese press was the first to leak the news of Chan's secret marriage to Lin, and this news sent a Japanese girl to her death when in despair she threw herself in front of a train. A Chinese girl even tried to commit suicide in front of Chan's own offices in Kowloon. Chan was quoted as saying, "I have to be responsible for my fans." He has been romantically linked with a number of his female costars, including Maggie Cheung and Anita Mui, but no one can say anything. Chan's people stay very close protecting his privacy. A girlfriend cannot walk with him or be seen in public. Their safety depends on their anonymity. It's no wonder that Chan is usually surrounded by many different women when his picture is taken. With so much heartache stemming from his personal revelations, Chan doesn't need any more.

In his heart and in his mind, Jackie Chan is an international entertainer, plain and simple.

Favorite leading lady Maggie Cheung in *Twin Dragons.*
(*Colin Geddes/Asian Eye. By permission of Media Asia Group. © STAR TV*))

films for other stars and directors, whose talents and goals perhaps lay outside of his own visions and dreams. Chan's first feature with Golden Way was *Naughty Boys* (1986), a light comedy using Chan's famous stunt team to balance the humor with two fantastic action scenes. The finale, set inside a warehouse, boasts some of the best Buster Keaton–type action this side of Chan himself. He does appear at the beginning in a brief shot, and the end credit sequence shows Chan performing a stunt for Shaw Brothers queen Hui Ying-hung. The film also gave Chan's longtime stuntman friend Mars a lead role.

In 1986 Chan worked with Stanley Kwan, who picked up an assistant director's job on *Armour of God* after his own directorial outings had not hit pay dirt. Kwan was to become one of the most sought-after art directors after helming *Rouge* (1987) and *Actress* (1992), both of which Chan produced. *Rouge* also gave Hong Kong pop singer Anita Mui the chance to flex her acting muscle, and she won the Best Actress award for her role at the eighth annual Hong Kong Film Awards. Chan would use Mui in three films: *Mr. Canton and Lady Rose, Drunken Master II,* and *Rumble in the Bronx.* Because of the acclaim for her performance in *Actress* (or *Center Stage*), Maggie Cheung would also enjoy a long career outside of leading lady roles. She won praise for playing herself in the French film *Irma Vep* (1996).

Two other productions that Chan is known for are the *Inspector Wears Skirts* series, both of which are entries in the femme fatale genre. American martial arts movie queen Cynthia Rothrock appeared in the first film, also known as *Top Squad*. "Everyone always says, 'She's the female Van Damme' or 'She's the female Chuck Norris,' or 'She's the female Bruce Lee,' which isn't too bad. But if I had it my way, I would like to be compared to Jackie Chan," said Rothrock. Like *Naughty Boys*, these films feature Chan's trademark action, putting his stunt team in the forefront.

Jackie Chan isn't a part of Hong Kong cinema—Hong Kong cinema is a part of Jackie

Jackie Chan, Willie Chan, and Stanley Tong on the set of *First Strike.* (*Courtesy of Golden Harvest*)

Chan. Without him the industry would have been dead years ago, fallen victim to Hollywood's product. Chan is the life force of the Asian film world, and this is perhaps the reason that he will never leave. They never turned their backs on him, and they have adored him for close to three decades. Chan's contribution to Hong Kong cinema's well-being is unique—certainly no American filmmaker has a similar role in Hollywood. Jackie Chan is the president of both the Hong Kong Motion Picture Association and the Hong Kong Director's Guild and the honorary president of the Hong Kong Society of Cinematographers. He is also the vice president of the Hong Kong Performance Artiste Guild and serves on the executive committee of the Hong Kong Stuntman's Association. In fact, *Twin Dragons* was made in an effort to raise money for the Hong Kong Director's Guild, just as *Drunken Master II* was made to fund new headquarters for the Hong Kong Stuntman's Association.

It is also an unspoken pledge that Jackie Chan will personally take care of all the expenses of any stuntman who is injured on one of his films. Whereas some injured Hollywood stuntmen have had to go to court for compensation. Chan wouldn't even blink over such a matter. "As far as I know, no one in Jackie's team has

$35,000,000

龍兄虎弟 打破全港紀錄

謹向全港觀眾致謝 同業互勉

最後今天
決不展期

Hong Kong newspaper ad taken by Jackie Chan. He's thank-ing his fans for *Armour of God*'s HK $35 million gross. (*Colin Geddes/Asian Eye*)

the triads' reign of terror. The triads are Hong Kong criminal organizations whose illegal activities have spilled over into the bustling film industry (although some triads conduct legitimate business). The "Showbusiness Against Violence" banner that lead the way for these harassed stars eventually took them to police headquarters, where a department called O.C.T.B. (Organized Crime and Triad Bureau) exists. At first, the triads just demanded protection money, but their stranglehold on the cinematic community gradually tightened. At one time Jackie Chan's manager, Willie Chan, had more than forty clients working for him. The triads took nearly everyone away, and today, he manages only a select few aside from Jackie Chan: Kenneth Low Houi-kang (Jackie's bodyguard), Michael Wong Mun-tak (*City Hunter, Thunderbolt*), and Rosamund Kwan Chi-lam (*Armour of God, Project A II*).

The once-vibrant Hong Kong cinema has experienced a downward spiral of quality in the past three years (1993 was the last "good" year, at that). In Hong Kong, Hollywood films actually began to outsell its own, whereas it was formerly theorized that Hong Kong's audiences couldn't be tempted by Tinseltown. "Escapism, a universal reason for movie attendance, has been an all-consuming passion of Hong Kong filmgoers, whether it be escapism from crowded living conditions, from ideological battles or from the prospect of 1997 [Hong Kong's reunification with Mainland China]," writes John Lent in his study, *The Asian Film Industry*. The New Wave directors that led the resurgence of popularity of Hong Kong cinema were even beginning to stumble, working outside their own styles. The same actors and actresses began showing up in every production. Some actors make over twelve films in a given year! Audiences were just plain tired of seeing the same faces, and since the films were retreading Hollywood films, they simply

ever suffered permanent handicaps," says Hong Kong stuntman James Ha. "Accidents do occur in our business, and there were a few rare instances in which stuntpeople were killed or became handicapped, but none with Jackie. For stuntpeople who had accidents, Jackie had always been eager to show his support in any way he could, even those who were not in his personal team."

On January 15, 1992, Chan made a bold move by marching with over three hundred members of the film industry in an effort to end turned to the sources themselves.

The one bright star in Hong Kong's cinema's gloomy future is Jackie Chan. He is and always will be Asia's biggest superstar. Whether his films will be shot in English or any other language, it makes little difference. In Hong Kong *Rumble in the Bronx* easily outgrossed every other film from 1995, even though over forty percent of the film was in English.

With this kind of stardom, Chan currently earns HK $15 million per film, but bonuses and royalties push that earning to HK $30 million (about US $5 million). And with investments in Hong Kong, Singapore, Australia, and the United States, Chan has an estimated worth of $40 million—maybe more.

Certainly, Chan is Golden Harvest's biggest investment—they can't afford to lose him. Years ago, they needed each other, but he is now finding it difficult to resist Hollywood's overtures—despite his cultural ties to Hong Kong, which he has always honored. As a result, in 1996 Golden Harvest began grooming a possible Chan replacement, Aaron Kwok Fu-sing, a handsome young actor and pop star. Without a martial arts background, Kwok has many years to go before maturing as an action star. Still, he was paid $10 million in a four-picture deal promising the same kind of budgets Chan has on his blockbusters. Kwok's first film was *Somebody Up There Likes Me* (1996), where he played a kick-boxer coached by none other than Sammo

Chan clowns around on the set of *Rumble in the Bronx.* Stuntman Alan Sit is on the right. (*Courtesy of Golden Harvest*)

Hung. In an interview with Hong Kong's *Sing Tao Daily*, Chan commented on Kwok: "I don't worry about this. Golden Harvest has one more person to use, which makes me happy. I don't feel Kwok is my replacement. My replacement must be young—fourteen or fifteen years old would be best."

With Golden Way and Jackie and Willie Productions (the business office that represents his interests), Chan is too busy to worry about replacements, anyway. Even so, he always remembers the fans who keep him at the top. In 1996, Media Asia, who distributes all of Chan's films, shot a documentary on Chan's life in the cinema. Chan had a say so in the filming, so anything that might be considered negative was excised. But for his diehard fans hungry for information about him, Jackie Chan will do anything. That same year, for the US fan club's birthday, Chan had his secretary videotape a tour through the beautifully designed Jackie and Willie offices. You can sense the urgency of everything he does: Chan stops every few minutes to take a phone call or to eat—when he suddenly smells something good in the kitchen. The camera work and production values are not important, as Chan is simply showing his fans a normal day in his life. When Chan is not working on a film or traveling, his offices are generally considered his home.

Away from the screen, Chan is involved in a number of ventures. In Hong Kong, he has his

Chan with some of his many fans in Australia on the *Mr. Nice Guy* set. (*Courtesy of Jackie Chan Fan Club USA/Joy Al-Sofi*)

restraining the dimension of the action and revealing the weaknesses in the choreography. Since Hollywood directors spend little time on fight sequences, masters are easy to set up, and fight scenes can be shot in just a few hours.

Hong Kong directors rarely use master shots for fight sequences, opting for segment shooting instead. Although it takes longer to complete, segment shooting allows the director to shoot a number of movements, designed for only that shot, before moving the camera to repeat the process with a different set of movements. The lighting, the grips, and every other part of the filmmaking process has to be altered, as well, to keep the set's aesthetics in check. "They will do thirty or forty takes on parts of a fight, if necessary, and there is no master to a fight because they don't know after the first three or four techniques what the next movements will be," says Richard Norton.

All of Chan's fight sequences are achieved with segment shooting, and each fight takes over a month to complete. Typically, Chan will shoot a fight with a rather wide lens (18 to 35). After a few movements have been filmed, he will cut to a medium (50) or possibly a close-up (85), before he switches to another wide shot of the action to start the process all over again. A perfect example of this process is the first drinking scene in *Drunken Master II*. In between each segment of movements, Chan inserts medium shots of Anita Mui and her crew retrieving the alcohol for him to drink and cheering for him once the fight starts. These inserted shots are important because they show facial reactions, lighten the tone, and create transitions between the segments. This is how Chan shoots every single fight sequence. Chan doesn't use a lot of fancy camera techniques to enhance the action, because he wants the audience to see what is going on at all times. Chan's fight scenes suffer the most when they are not seen in the correct aspect ratio of 2.35:1, known as the scope format. The composition of the fight is completely ruined if it is not seen in this ratio.

Sammo Hung has been called the best action director around because he can quickly direct and choreograph a scene, while using dif-

ferent techniques to enhance the effects. Chan usually keeps the camera stationary when shooting a scene, but Hung uses a more experimental approach. He sets up a fight sequence with his trademark tracking shot, which circles the combatants and sets the tone for the battle at hand. It's anybody's guess as to what comes next, since Hung employs so many different techniques, like carefully placed overhead and low-angle shots. Hung will shoot in segments using wide angles, but many times he will shoot tighter with closer lenses, allowing him to concentrate more on the fighting techniques performed. "Sammo can set up a shot, shoot it, and move on to the next without any deliberation," remembers Chua Lam, a regular Hung collaborator.

Editing

Editing is the crucial element in tying together the direction and the choreography of the fight sequence. Often referred to as the montage, it is "the principle governing the organization of film elements, both visual and audio, or the combination of these elements, by juxtaposing them, connecting them, and/or controlling their duration." An editor who does not understand action can ultimately ruin the montage despite the director's and choreographer's talents.

Chan's segments and close or medium shots are linked with perfect accuracy, allowing the audience to see all of the action and gain insight into what the performers are feeling. The major distinction between Sammo Hung and Jackie Chan lies in the editing process. Chan's edits will signify changes in speed, but his cuts generally leave the action altogether for moments of subtlety. Hung on the other hand, slices and dices his action to speed up the intensity.

While both directors cut on the axis—whereby a singular shot of a kick or a punch will be carried over to another shot of where this movement will land—Hung does something entirely different. In Hung's fight scenes there are often many different groups of people fighting. Hung will cut on the axis, but the move will break the temporal plane, allowing the movement to actually carry over to another fight entirely. This moves the action along, creating a frenzy of intense camera work and keeping the audience on its toes. Hung's most impressive and innovative fight sequence to date is the fight in the pachinko parlor in *Thunderbolt* (1995). Many fans were turned off by the varying camera angles and speeds and the use of wires, but the action is edited to perfection. The colorful set also gave the fight more dimension, and Hung was able to employ different fighting styles (such as sumo wrestling) since the battle takes place in Japan.

To summarize the filmmaking process in a Hollywood scenario, the director, fight choreographer, and editor usually can't make a fight scene work. The lack of synergy between the three is part ego, part misunderstanding, and part lack of effort. The Hong Kong scenario is quite different because the director, fight choreographer, and editor all understand the process, and, often, are one and the same person. Editing isn't saved for the end of the shoot; it's done right on the spot to keep the constant flow of ideas fresh and coherent. If a director does not know how to shoot action, an action director is hired to do just that.

British martial arts actor Gary Daniels has been trying to crack the American scene for the past few years, but he has come to realize that only Hong Kong can really bring out his qualities as a martial arts actor. He was supposed to film an $8-million American production in Africa with a group of other martial arts heavies but instead took a small-budget film entitled *Blood Moon* for Ng See-yuen. The reason? Instead of filming another lackluster martial arts effort, Daniels wanted the chance to have another film (other than *City Hunter*) under his belt that showed the proper relationship between direction, choreography, and editing.

In understanding the difference in regards to Chan, watch the end fight sequence in the Hollywood version of *The Protector,* then in the Chinese version. Chan didn't have the time to reshoot everything, but watch how his editing, direction, and choreography make the scene infinitely better than the Glickenhaus version. Hong Kong films may never have huge budgets to work with, but they will never be championed in terms of detailing the best action scenes around.

Humor

To keep the action genre more in the mainstream, humor is inserted to lighten the tone. Comedic elements vary in style between America, Jackie Chan, and Sammo Hung. One-liners shape the Hollywood style, though they set up a striking contradiction in tone. In *Lethal Weapon,* for instance, Danny Glover and Mel Gibson bounce off endless one-liners, making the audience laugh, then in seconds, they pull out their guns and start blowing people away, with blood going everywhere. Technically, the comedy and the action are never taking place at exactly the same time, but one can't help but see the drastic tonal change from good-hearted fun to supposed heroic bloodshed.

One-liners do not exist in Hong Kong action films at all, thankfully. Jackie Chan creates comic gestures in the implausibility of the movements themselves. In a real fight no one would perform acrobatics or stand there and kick forever. The fights are long and exhausting and without anyone actually getting killed or bleeding to death. This brings up an interesting conception of the American public in relation to the length of fight sequences. Keith Vitali explains: "The biggest difference between a Hong Kong fight scene and an American fight scene is the display of power. That's why Steven Seagal is so popular. He throws one powerful movement, and that person goes to the ground. In Hong Kong films, someone could jump up and throw a powerful side kick, but the person would just get right back up. Americans take this difference so literally."

When Bruce Lee came on the screen, there was no chance of his going down or getting defeated. If he kicked or hit you, that was it. In Chan's quest to lighten everything up, he stages incredibly choreographed fight sequences where the participants really don't have a pain threshold. While realism is somewhat diminished because of how long a scene lasts, it still does seem to exist because the fighters are doing everything in wide-angle shots right in front of the audience.

Do people pay to see Seagal act or fight? If they pay to see him fight, then why do they have to watch ninety minutes of dialogue just to see a total of five minutes of fighting? It doesn't make any sense. If one can get over the fact that Chan's scenes are "implausibly realistic," at least the audience is treated to seeing him and his stunt team perform a myriad of moves for ten-minute intervals.

In *Rumble in the Bronx*, the scene where Chan gets pummeled with bottles actually created quite a controversy for Stanley Tong and Chan because the scene used blood. Usually, the only blood in a Chan film is in the out-take sequence, and there was much debate about whether to have it in the scene—always keeping the family audience in mind. But Tong explains their final decision: "We had to have something to show how bad [gangs] are. . . . If we don't put blood, it doesn't look right." Much of the brutality of this scene was inspired by Tong and Chan's real-life experiences with Hong Kong street violence.

Chan usually tries to keep things light by siphoning the violence out of the action. His other way to lighten the tone of the action is by facial expressions. Classic tough guys broodingly rip into their opponents, and if they get hit, they take it in stride. Since Chan is an underdog, though, his characteristics have to be more human, not like a stone-faced fighter. In *First Strike* when he gets his hand stuck in the hinge of a ladder, he pulls his hand away and makes pained gestures to the audience. Taking method acting to a new level, when Chan eats the Chinese red peppers in *Project A II*, his face turns bright red with anguish, as one can see the effects of the peppers in his mouth. In every fight scene, the audience has to see what Chan is

feeling, and they know he is not supposed to be the tough guy. "I can't tell you of an American fighter that has as good of a facial expression than Jackie Chan on the screen. They just don't show it," says Keith Vitali.

From a filmmaking standpoint, Chan doesn't rely on much editing, because it would increase the intensity. Editing creates the perception of a scene's being more violent than what was originally shot. Chan's scenes are intense enough, and he keeps everything in wide shots so that they appear like miniature circus acts. The music never has a lot of heart-pounding bass to accent the danger. In Chan's films the music is like a dance number played out as a background melody, accenting only the rhythm of the movement.

Sammo Hung, on the other hand, has a completely different take on the matter. His fight sequences do show a display of power. If they are long, they are broken down to offset the length. Hung does show blood and bruises to convey pain, but he does not fill his scenes with outlandish movements. He keeps things realistic, so the characters in his films must provide the touches of humor. Hung's most classic film to use this element is in his 1990 masterpiece *Pedicab Driver*. At the end of the film, Hung comes upon a group of men who are all eating rice. After setting up the stage of the fight, the camera pans across the men, who are still chewing their food. The camera then cuts to the overweight Hung, who is licking his lips. The montage of shots that follow shows Hung kicking and smashing his opponents with everything he has, forcing the mouths of his enemies to spew up speckles of rice. It's an awkward approach, but this is how Hung lightens his action. Other Hung examples of humor include Yuen Wah's cigar chomping in *Dragons Forever* and James Tien's caustic laugh in *Heart of Dragon*.

Hung likes to carry out his fight scenes without music. If music does exist, though, it is accented with booming bass, signifying the power of the scene. At the end of *Heart of Dragon* (Japanese version), music is entirely left out, with the exception of a crackling beat to mark Chan's shooting of a man at the top of a stairway.

Chan's filmmaking style and use of comedy have made his action films the best in the world, but he personally adds one more aspect to them that separates them from the rest. Chan realized that many on his crew and among his Peking Opera brothers could fight as well as perform acrobatics. He wanted to come up with something different.

He did it after his fight inside the clock tower in *Project A*. In a single moment Jackie Chan would break himself from the mold in which men are made, and become an incredibly different animal. With four cameras set up, Chan would do Harold Lloyd one better by falling some fifty feet below from the clock tower. "For seven days, I couldn't do it. Every day I would dangle with a stuntman close by. Everyone would just stand there watching me. I was scared. On the last day the stuntman did not wait around, and I couldn't go back in," said Chan during the U.S. publicity tour for *Rumble*. When Chan finally let go of the clock hand, he tumbled through two awnings and landed on the ground. He shot that scene not only once, but several times, with three versions making the final cut of the film. Chan did the fall in one shot—in an American film a fall like this would have been edited with three shots to mask the stunt mattress below. The practice of shooting a spectacular stunt in one shot (no cheating with edits) became a trademark of the Jackie Chan stunt scene. It wouldn't work any other way.

The stunt he is most known for, however, is not this fall from the clock tower but the relatively easy jump onto a tree at the beginning of *Armour of God*. Chan had done the jump correctly the first time, but ever the perfectionist, he wanted one more just in case. When the branch broke, Chan plummeted to the ground, the European cameraman scurrying out of his way. Chan landed headfirst on a rock. "I was twenty meters away, and everyone was silent on

No tough guy: Chan in *Mr. Canton and Lady Rose.* (By permission of Media Asia Group. © STAR TV)

the set," said Chua Lam, one of the film's producers. "We rushed down, noticing that Chan was not bleeding at all, but when we got to him and pulled him up, blood was pouring out of his ears." Fact is, the rock pierced Chan's skull. Chan went to a Yugoslavian hospital for two weeks, then he went to Paris to see an American doctor for another ten days. When Chan returned to the set, he was as good as new and showed no signs of his near-fatal fall. Ironically, Chan was hurt by a simple stunt—a lesson he will never forget.

It's important to mention that many Hong Kong stuntmen and actors are just plain crazy when it comes to displaying their physical abilities in the cinema. In a no-budget action film entitled *Tiger on Beat II*, actor Conan Lee made a jump onto a light pole, slipped, and fell straight to the ground. Although it was an accident, the fall makes Chan's drop in *Project A* look like child's play. Many actors and actresses do their own stunts because insurance and unions are not as obligatory to the production as in American films.

Chan and Hung are both very physically demanding on the actors and actresses that

Sammo Hung runs through the choreography with Chan and Urquidez. (*Courtesy of Sara Urquidez*).

lighter tone to balance out the faster segments.

Since they are fighting in a room, Chan kicks a long bench out of the way. This indicates that the two are going to fight it out without any obstacles. A large, red rug makes it almost look as if the two were fighting in a ring without ropes. The camera then pans around to the side while both men begin to circle one other to set up their strategies. While the fight is in motion, fake-outs are used to set up real maneuvers right after them.

A clever gag in the film displays the power that the audience needs to see for believability. When Urquidez pushes Chan against a table, inching him back step by step, he throws a spinning round heel kick, only to miss Chan and blow out the candles that are on the table behind him. "By the time I had to shoot that scene, I was so tired that I could only blow out one or two of the six candles. Finally, the crew came up with an idea. At the same time that I spun around, there was someone with a piece of cardboard to catch any of the remaining candles that were still lit. Believe it or not, I was able to blow them all out by myself. I spun so hard that I almost twisted my back, because I just wanted to get to the next scene."

American fight choreography are solved by using the subtleties of real combat: the mannerisms, setting the stage, strategizing, and creating a rhythmic trading of blows. Segment shooting, slow-motion shots, panning, and undercranking the camera are all used in Hung's resume, edited to a breakneck pace. Hung breaks the fight up into three parts, which gives the audience what it wants without drawing the realism away by presenting a long, improbable encounter. The final element to this fight is Hung's clear understanding of fighting techniques and how they relate to specific body types.

Each character is given various mannerisms in preparation. Urquidez takes off his coat and strums his suspenders while staring down Chan. As the fight progresses, he licks his lips and shakes his hands to keep loose for the bout at hand. Chan pulls off his shirt, does some knee bends, dances around a bit, and stretches out. Since Urquidez is a real fighter, Hung lets him fight as such, without weakening facial expressions, which would let his enemy know that he was injured. On the other hand, Chan grunts, wiggles his nose, and rubs his head to remedy the pain. The fight is thus given moments of

(*Courtesy of Sara Urquidez*)

Vitali gets a taste of his own medicine thanks to Yuen Biao. (*Colin Geddes/Asian Eye. By permission of Media Asia Group. © STAR TV*)

The fight itself was mapped out by Sammo Hung, who let both Chan and Urquidez use their appropriate skills. Benny "the Jet" Urquidez is undoubtedly the best ring fighter the world has ever seen. He was one of the most prominent kickboxers to bring traditional American boxing to the foundation of martial arts. Urquidez keeps a fairly small base, bending his knees to keep a powerful stance. In watching the scene, notice his leg movements, which spring out from the sharp rise of his knees. He also mixes it up with direct punching and powerful elbow and knee techniques. Chan's stance is a little wider so that he can aim his kicks higher.

Though the scene was choreographed, Urquidez is quick to mention the little agreement between Chan and himself: "I remember Jackie asking me if I was a real fighter. I said yes, and then he replied, 'Well, how hard can I hit you?' 'Well, I'm used to taking a lot of impact, so it depends on how real you want to make it.' Jackie said, 'I want it to be real!' 'How real?' 'As real as possible?' 'Well, I'm game for it if you are.' We agreed that the fight was to be a give-and-take situation." After working out together and fighting each other in two scenes prior to the climax, the two were ready to duke it out without any pulled punches. "We actually slept right there on the stage and fought that scene over the course of five days. After we rested, we would get up and go at it again. I became so involved with the fight that sometimes I forgot I was filming a movie!"

Keith Vitali, who fought Yuen Biao in the climax, remembers that Chan and Urquidez did get a little heated during their confrontation. The fact that Vitali and Urquidez, both professional fighters, hit hard was something they did not expect would agitate the crew. "They had to get their revenge," Vitali remembers. "In my scene, Yuen Biao throws wine in my face. As the wine is stinging my eyes, he crashes a real ceramic vase over my head. When you're watching the scene, notice the smile as I fall backward. That wasn't acting; I was laughing to myself in astonishment that they used a real vase to literally knock me unconscious!"

Urquidez would not get away so easily. In one of the final segments, a rather tight shot shows Urquidez being clobbered with Chan's clenched fists inside leather gloves. In a grueling fifteen takes, Chan was literally hitting Urquidez with everything he had. "I asked Benny if he was okay, and all he said was, 'No problem!' Benny is a superman when it comes to pain," says Vitali.

(*Courtesy of Sara Urquidez*)

Whang Inn-sik catches Chan off-guard when quenching his thirst. *Young Master.* (*Colin Geddes/Asian Eye. By permission of Media Asia Group. © STAR TV*)

American fight choreographers should take note of the complexities of this spectacular montage of camerawork, fighting techniques, and the war itself.

2. *Young Master* (1980): Jackie Chan vs. Whang Inn-sik 2.35:1

This period kung fu film's finale ranks as having the best segment shooting with wide angles. In all the martial arts films ever made, the Korean style of hapkido has never looked better. Unlike the multitudes of kung fu fight sequences, this isn't a bloodthirsty rite of revenge but merely an exhibition. Halfway into the film, the audience can see the power of Whang's kicks, but his character seems to take on a monstrous form, with long, ugly hair, ragged clothes, and beady eyes. When Chan confronts him to save his friend at the end, Whang looks like an ordinary person, with nicely combed hair and appropriate attire. Thus, the scene isn't trying to pit good guy versus bad guy in the traditional sense; fighting Whang is just something that Chan has to do. When Chan needs a drink of water or a quick rest, Whang just waits idly by until his opponent is ready to

engage again. The intensity of the matchup is not an important factor, so fast-paced editing isn't necessary. Instead the match is shot in extremely wide angles, as if to show the audience a demonstration.

And that's precisely what Master Whang Inn-sik was doing. Hapkido practitioner Whang demonstrates all three components of the form: the traditional kicks of karate, the throws of judo, and the wrist and arm manipulations of aikido. Hapkido was actually taken from Daito-ryu aiki-jujitsu, the same style from which aikido was created. Most of the combative measures of the art are not tapped into because Chan just isn't a worthy match. Whang does use the cat stance, one of the key elements of the style. The stance has the participant keep the front leg off the ground at all times; after any kick is thrown, the leg simply moves back to that position. Whang hops at Chan, shooting his front leg at him with lightning speed, even dropping it occasionally to let the back leg get in a kick or two.

After assaulting him with kicks, Whang then moves to wrist manipulations, flipping Chan around as though he were a puppet. By applying pressure on the elbow, he works Chan over with variations of arm bars and painful wrist and hand contortions. At one point, Chan becomes so infuriatingly helpless that he jumps up and down screaming, trying to make Whang let go. Minutes of torture go by until Whang decides to go one step further with his holds by actually throwing him to the ground, still clutching the leverage points.

When Whang was kicking, Chan grabbed hold of his legs. When Whang started throwing him around, Chan grabbed hold of his body. The first fifteen minutes of this fight are spent giving Chan a lesson in the art of hapkido. One of the major flaws in many martial art fight scenes is when the good guy suddenly develops the ability to overcome the villainous opponent who had been winning the fight all along. But in *Young Master,* Chan doesn't come back with some new style of kung fu. In fact, his body is so numb from the beating he is enduring that he just stands up for more punishment. With a confused look on his face, Whang continues the assault once again, but this time, Chan isn't going down. He stands with an empty look on his face letting Whang kick him in the chest and face as hard as he can. Even more surprisingly, when Whang does get the upper hand, throwing him around like a rag doll, Chan walks away only to throw himself down in repeated intervals, showing that he can't be injured anymore!

By running at Whang like a lunatic, Chan kicks, head-butts, pinches, and punches Whang, who finally gets a taste of his own medicine. When Whang grabs him, Chan starts kicking his legs until Whang lets go. When Whang throws him on the ground, Chan tries to fight him from the ground. In the end Chan breaks Whang's back by folding his legs over the top him. He has apparently won the duel, but Chan's crazed demeanor doesn't stop there. Like a lion who toys with his deceased prey, Chan grabs Whang and thrashes him back and forth until his aggression has faded away.

The scene took over three months to shoot, and Whang and Chan would work out together morning, noon, and night to pull off ten filmed actions a day! The camera showcases the two executing countless movements of action before an alternate angle is inserted. There isn't anything in the setting to get in the way of the fight, as they are dueling it out on a flat grassland prairie.

Some of the kicks in the film were push kicks, which means that Chan actually met Whang's foot without receiving the impact of the force behind it. With the wide-angle shots, several cable jerks pulled the recipient of the kick from one side of the shot to the other. A cable jerk uses a cable attached to a harness fastened from the neck to the abdomen for support. One method, clearly the one used in this film, is to have about ten men just jerk the cable, pulling the person as if he or she was shot with a shotgun or kicked by Whang Inn-sik.

One of the best things about this fight is the accompanying classical music, *The Planets,* a suite by Holst. Also, the fight must be seen in wide screen to get the full effect of the techniques. Indirectly learning from Master Whang, Chan has often credited hapkido as being part of his martial arts foundation. Watching Whang in action, it's easy to see why. (Chan currently trains with a hapkido master.) Whang presently resides in Canada, where he heads up the Eagle Hapkido Academy, still teaching in his sixties.

3. *Heart of Dragon* (1985): Jackie Chan vs. Dick Wei and Company 1.85:1

This represents a rare opportunity to see Chan as an offensive fighter. He's not running away from anything, and everyone who comes into his path better watch out. With Sammo Hung at the helm, Chan's potential brutality is finally unleashed without the light melodies and touches of humor that his own scenes possess. The final fight scene in *Heart of Dragon* is without a doubt the best use of editing and set design in Hung's resume. Amid damp floors littered with boards and the odds and ends of a construction site, Chan and his crew must take on the seedy criminals that lurk behind every nook and cranny of a multilevel building. Chan's part in the action is played during the middle, while his buddies shoot machine guns and blow up grenades on both ends.

With the flickering sparks of welding slicing the dark air, Chan works his way through the lower level in an uncomfortable haste. The first sign that this is not your typical Chan fight scene comes when a man holding a shovel greets him at the top of some stairs. Chan doesn't try to fight his way past—he just pulls the trigger and blows him away. Without any warning, a combatant surprises Chan at every turn, using various weapons. Instead of fighting all of these people, Chan's violent edge gets the best of him as he puts a machete through a guy's neck, slams a pickax into someone's stomach, and pierces a foe's chest with a sharp steel rod. The manic look on Chan's face is mesmerizing, as he becomes a dangerous character instead of a character who reacts in dangerous situations.

At one turn Chan is ambushed by Dick Wei in their fourth, and best, knock-down-and-drag-out scene together. Allowing no time for setting the mood or strategy, Hung match-cuts this fantastic duel with complete cohesiveness. The fight takes place in three different parts,

Chan and Benny Lai, *Police Story II.* (*Media Asia Group.*
© *STAR TV*)

down to the ground when the drug takes effect.
Though Yuen was one of Chan's Peking Opera
brothers, he prided himself on having learned
Ying Jow Pai, otherwise known as Eagle Claw.
Hung was definitely making a comical reference
to this style.

All of the action in this sequence is top-
notch, and it has made *Dragons Forever* one of
the most classic fight films of the eighties.

8. *Police Story II* (1988): Jackie Chan vs. Benny Lai 2.35:1

Chan has no problem defeating Koo's men
for a second time or the mad bombers during
numerous skirmishes. When you watch him in
action, it's almost as if a little bit of Steven
Seagal's or Bruce Lee's no-nonsense tough guys
had rubbed off on him. In Chan's world, however, he can never truly be shown as the best
fighter, especially when he tries to take on
stuntman-friend Benny Lai in the film's final
moments.

During the middle of *Police Story II*, when
Chan and one of his cohorts discover the
bomber's lair and Lai's deaf character for the
first time, they show sympathy for him in the
way they try to communicate that he's under
arrest. They completely lose any thought that a
deaf person could pose any threat to either one
of them. Within a few seconds, though, Lai
jumps off the side of the wall, has both of them
down, and is able to make his escape without
any conflict.

After disposing of the gang's other two
members inside of a fireworks warehouse, Chan
is once again confronted with Lai, who demon-

strates his abilities by jumping up into the air
and kicking him three times all in one shot!
While Chan is unsuccessfully trying to fight
him, the camera keeps cutting to his astonished
face as he tries to wipe the sweat off his brow.
Not one time during this entire matchup does
Chan even land one punch or kick. He tries to
fake Lai out by climbing on the underside of
some steps, displaying an incredible show of
strength, but Lai is waiting at every turn. Chan
finally tries to escape his clutches, but when he
comes upon a crate full of small firecrackers,
Chan decides to give Lai a piece of his own
medicine. While Lai can't actually talk in the
film, he makes these bizarre, little animal
sounds. Chan mimics him when he gets
the upper hand, pelting him with the flame-
inducing firecrackers.

No American star would ever let such a
beating take place without physically coming
back at the end. Chan's ironic finale puts a
dampening effect on the pretentious behavior
his character had exhibited during the course of
the film.

9. *Drunken Master* (1979): Jackie Chan vs. Hwang Jang-lee 2.35:1

Chan's second fight with Korean boot-
kicker Hwang Jang-lee is a classic test between
the Eight Drunken Fairies and the traditional
use of tae kwon do. Chan uses all eight tech-

Hwang Jang-lee in action with Chan. *Drunken Master.* (*Colin
Geddes/Asian Eye*)

(By permission of Media Asia Group. © STAR TV)

Honorable Mention goes to *Armour of God*'s fight with the monks, *Drunken Master II*'s duel with Lau Kar-leung under a train, *Project A II*'s fight with Chan Wei-man and Wang Lung-wei, and finally *Dragons Forever*'s three-way battle between Jackie Chan, Sammo Hung, and Yuen Biao.

niques learned from his "drunken" teacher, played by Simon Yuen. The stance for the drunken style has the participant outstretch his arms and curl the fingers toward the body as if holding a cup (of alcohol). By doing so, the ball of the wrist is exposed, allowing the user to unleash what is commonly called an ox strike or crane technique. This move is used only in close encounters.

As for Hwang, he sticks to more of the traditional tae kwon do, which means the art of kicking and punching. Tae kwon do has become watered down in the States, having been made popular by competition. When the art was first developed, it was more of a complete system utilizing open hand movements, wrist locks, and throws. And Hwang Jang-lee was a definite traditionalist, learning from within the origins of the art. He uses an open hand almost the entire time in this bout with Chan and performs some of his trademark high-kicking techniques. If Americans think that Jean-Claude Van Damme is a great kicker, one look at Hwang Jang-lee's abilities will surely make anyone forget about the Muscles from Brussels! Hwang's amazing footwork was so popular that he was invited to make a documentary called *The Art of High Impact Kicking* during the early eighties.

The fifteen-minute battle in *Drunken Master* is one of director Yuen Woo-ping's most famous fight sequences, and Chan's handling of the drunken style is both comical and seemingly useful.

10. *Police Story II* (1988): Jackie Chan vs. Koo's henchmen on the playground 2.35:1

It was just a walk in the park for Chan, as he and Maggie Cheung were trying to work out their differences as a couple. Koo's right-hand man had different plans for him, however, when he lures him onto a playground. A fight ensues, pitting Chan against his stuntmen in a grueling session of pain as they battle it out around a swing set, a slide, and other playground objects. What makes this fight more stunning than the rest of his ensemble matches is his stuntmen. Usually, Chan stands out as being a scene's only combatant to use unconventional fighting skills to overcome his opponents, but this fight has everyone flipping, jumping, and orchestrating their bodies. It's hard to keep your eyes just on Chan as many of his stuntmen are performing some of the better flips and flops. Like all of the fight sequences in *Police Story II*, they are overly sped up for some reason, but this doesn't detract from the audience's excitement in watching these truly gifted individuals duke it out with fists, feet, and metal rods, which seem to come out of nowhere. In one shot Chan runs up the side of a swing set, slapping his stick on the top of one of his stuntman's heads.

When Chan is almost crushed by the enemy car that corners him in an alley, the music really picks up to show that Chan is going to turn things around. In one of his fight's more comical moments, he tries to pick up a drainage pipe; the menacing scowl on his face is suddenly reduced to a look of embarrassment when he can't even budge it.

Sadly, *Police Story II* has never been released in a complete letterbox on videotape in any language. (There is a Japanese laser disc, but no other.) This fight as well as all of the other action scenes are left to suffer.

Jackie's Sensational Seven

All of Jackie Chan's films have their positive qualities, so it's difficult to pick his best films when there is so much to like in all of them. My list has been narrowed down to Chan's definitive seven. Keep in mind that all of these films were analyzed and judged in their original Chinese formats. The only readily available copy of *Mr. Canton and Lady Rose* in English is missing more than thirty minutes of footage, and the lack of letterboxing would send it to the very bottom of the list, compared to the standing it has here. Hopefully, this book and other sources will finally get ambitious video companies to release these films the way they were meant to be seen.

1. *Project A II* (1987)

This is Chan's grand achievement, showcasing all of his trademarks within a firm story and multiple plot lines. While it lacks the gloss of his *Mr. Canton and Lady Rose* (1989), it more than makes up for it with scene after scene of original and inspired bits, both physical and comedic. Chan returns as the heroic Dragon Ma, who had rid the China seas of pirates in *Project A* (1983). When a crooked police superintendent is exposed publicly, Ma is pulled away from his mariner duties and assigned to take over the west side of the superintendent's precinct—the most troubled area, of course. Before the film can expand on the basic plotline of Ma's cleaning house of the shady

Chan defends Dodo Cheng in *Armour of God II: Operation Condor*. (*Colin Geddes/Asian Eye. By permission of Media Asia Group. © STAR TV*)

Chan's triumphant return as Dragon Ma—here, on a ledge with Rosamund Kwan. (*Colin Geddes/Asian Eye. By permission of Media Asia Group. © STAR TV*)

police force, a second subplot introduces a group of revolutionaries bent on staging a coup to return China back to its traditional roots. And more trouble arises when the government sends its own henchmen to seek out and murder these traitors before they can take arms. As a comedic accent, a minor subplot adds "the ax gang," a bunch of disgruntled pirates who owe their hardships to Ma for killing their captain in the first film. Tying *Project A II* together, the superintendent shows up at every turn to make deals with opposing sides for monetary gain, discrediting Ma in the process.

The greatest scene in this film—in any of Chan's films—pulls together all of these subplots into one incredible predicament. The scene starts when two of the government henchmen kidnap a revolutionary and take her back to her apartment to find a book containing all of the revolutionaries' names. Then the cousin of the revolutionary comes home to find Ma and another cop (handcuffed together because Ma is set up at the film's beginning) at her doorstep, sending the other three in hiding. When the police commissioner (Bill Tung) arrives, Ma and company must also go into hiding, putting the

cousin in a very tight spot. After the commissioner becomes soaked in water in fixing a leaky faucet, he puts on a woman's blouse to keep warm and subsequently handcuffs himself to a sofa while showing off. Of course, he can't find the key because Ma took it to release himself when the commissioner's clothes were removed during the faucet situation. Along comes the crafty superintendent for a spell to create even more commotion in this complex hide-and-go-seek game.

The scene took ten days just to prepare. Chan explains, "One month! It took one month to shoot that scene. I'm just sitting there—who goes in first? Who's hiding? OK, let's do this. This isn't right—OK, Maggie [cousin of the revolutionary] comes out. No, wait—I just keep thinking. Keep making, making, making." As the scene builds in momentum, the environment becomes so overloaded that it slowly begins to give each party a view of the other. The destruction of this game shows the sheer brilliance of Chan to coherently direct a scene of this complexity.

Chan's stunt crew is also in full force, putting together several great action pieces—the first being Ma's onslaught on one of the West side's most feared crime lords. A melee of brawling and acrobatic fist and footwork incorporates Chan's fixation with making the environment—with its tables, chairs, and ladders—an active

Chan and his most famous leading lady, Maggie Cheung. (*Colin Geddes/Asian Eye. By permission of Media Asia Group. © STAR TV*)

Ti Lung.

Anita Mui.

his father would. In every scene she's in, Mui wins over the audience with her wisecracking tricks. Except for the kung-fu fighting females, women have always been underused in martial arts films, being nothing more than helpless, demure possessions. Mui's stepmother is caring and sweet, but she loves to play with her friends when her master is away, and she can fight if put to the test. She is so proud of her stepson that she encourages him to use his kung fu when his father forbids it.

Since the first *Drunken Master* was made sixteen years earlier, the biggest challenge for audiences was trying to accept the forty-one-year-old Chan as a twenty-something. Chan is completely believable in the role, and if his performance is compared to that of the first film, it really shows just how much of an actor Chan has become. By revitalizing the role with his charm, tenderness, and even sentiment, Chan's more rounded portrayal of Hwang Fei-hung is extremely entertaining to watch. The film only leaves a few minor mannerisms from the first film, like clasping the hands over the ears and kneeling at the first sign of father's disapproval. When Chan gets drunk, he looks the part instead of looking like he's merely playacting. When Chan cries for having disgraced his father, it's not a halfhearted effort, but one of gentleness. Chan's range of emotions in the film would of course have to include the conviction that all of his modern-day characters possess. In the end he must put aside his childish behavior to fight for not only his friends and family but for the preservation of his own culture.

Returning from a long journey, Chan and company must pass their possessions through customs to pay a tax. Hiding a container of ginseng (used for Hwang's medical practice) in the luggage of the upper-class passengers of a train, they bypass the tax—which Chan's father would disapprove of. When a mix-up occurs and Chan finds himself holding a rare jade seal instead, its disappearance sends the scheming tyrant in the British consulate into an uproar. The tyrant is using a steel mill as a cover for an operation to steal some of China's most precious treasures and sell them to the "London Museum." When they spot Chan in town, the tyrant's lackeys make trouble with him. On top of this, the tyrant wants the land that Po Chi Lam (the Hwang family medical practice) sits upon. When a retired, decorated Manchurian officer (Lau Kar-leung) comes to claim the seal and give back the ginseng, Chan learns the truth and must expose the powers that be.

In the beginning of the film, Chan plays the mischievous innocent of the first film. Instead of rebelling against traditionalism, Chan's character simply doesn't understand it. Before burning incense to show respect for his deceased mother, Chan happily jolts up the ladder to make the preparations. His father says in jest, "What's the hurry?" as if it were just another chore. When Chan gets into his first confrontation on the street and needs hard liquor to use drunken fist boxing, his father inscribes on a fan the words, "Water floats the boat but also capsizes the boat," referring to excessive drinking. When Lau comes for the seal, one of the servants is using it as a cutting stone. A conversation with Lau about the Chinese treasures teaches Chan their importance, and when Lau is killed, Chan stops at nothing to preserve their sanctity. Following the typical Chan mold, he knows that if the final onslaught on the mill and its thieving workers goes awry, he will have to pay with much more than mere repentance.

It's easy for fans to overlook the film's true merits of character development and relationships, because the action is in a class by itself. As in every Chan film, momentum must build to the finale, where Chan pulls out all the stops, sending the audience to its feet with excitement. The first fight scene takes place in the close quarters under the train, where Lau and Chan battle it out with a spear and sword, respectively.

The first drunken encounter is very Chaplinesque, with Chan bouncing from side to side, fighting off his enemies while trying to down bottles of liquor. In one shot Chan is almost lying flat while still keeping his feet on the ground! Most people believe this was done with a wire, but it's no cheat, and it pays homage to *Shaolin Wooden Men,* where he does the same trick. The leader of these lackeys is Ho Sung-park, a Korean tae kwon do expert. Ho is best known for portraying the Lo Kane character in the Mortal Kombat arcade game, and he can now be seen on the syndicated television series "Challenge of the Masters," a martial arts version of professional wrestling.

But sticking to styles is not Chan's way—it's Lau's—and by the end of the film, Chan needed to take over. The result is a fifteen-minute display of pure, raw Chan acrobatically fighting off Kenneth Low. It took four months to shoot this scene alone, and the result is worth it. More than any other Chan scene that comes to mind, the excitement put into this finale brings the audience to a new level of filmgoing experience. When Chan is kicked onto a 500°F hot bed of coals, he must drink industrial-strength alcohol to kill the pain and continue the fight. The slobberingly drunk Chan performs flips, breakdance moves, freestyle kung fu, and drunken boxing to defeat the lashing, nonstop kicks of Low. The camera work and choreography shows Chan's meticulous attention to detail, and the fact that the scene is not undercranked is proof that Chan isn't slowing down, despite his age.

The film's problems are in the editing of the film, where supposedly twenty minutes were cut. In the beginning a handsome son (Andy Lau) of a Chinese general is brought into the picture, but he disappears after the train sequence. When Lau

left as director, he took with him his own brother, who played one of Chan's friends, and Mark Houghton, the blonde-haired Brit who would have been one of Chan's major foes at the end of the film. Houghton is an amazing martial artist and Hong Kong action star, and he has trained under Lau for many years to learn Hung Gar. Also, when Chan enters the mill, he is supposed to rescue the kidnapped uncle of one of his friends. There wasn't any buildup, and the real problem at hand is to save the Chinese artifacts, so this makes little sense.

Despite these continuity problems, *Drunken Master II* gets better with every viewing. Luckily, it can be found anywhere in letterbox with subtitles by Tai Seng.

7. *Armour of God II: Operation Condor* (1991)

After *Mr. Canton and Lady Rose* went excessively over budget and failed to find its audience outside of Hong Kong, Chan needed to return to the security of his international hit *Armour of God.* Scriptwriter Edward Tang had a new story; Chan brought in two other mainstream directors (Johnny To and Frankie Chan) to work as assistants; and Raymond Chow had a deal: if Chan could finish the film in less than six months on a budget of HK $40 million, he would receive an additional bonus of HK $4 million.

By this time, however, Chan had become spoiled on the idea of larger productions, and after *Mr. Canton and Lady Rose,* there was no turning back. In the end he eclipsed the budget by more than HK $75 million—the final budget was a whopping HK $115 million (equivalent to US $15 million). As for meeting the shooting schedule, *Mr. Canton and Lady Rose* was released June 15, 1989, and *Armour of God II* was released February 7, 1991. Just as Golden Harvest was despairing, foreign film distributors went crazy with excitement over the sequel, and Chan came out great despite not releasing a film in 1990. "To this day, Jackie says that *Armour of*

God II was the most impressive production he has ever put together," says Edward Tang. What shows up on the screen couldn't have made fans any happier, with large-scale stunts, running sight gags, universal humor, and Chan's trademark fight sequences.

Changing his bird to Condor, Chan's new quest is to find an underground bunker where Germans from World War II supposedly hid billions of dollars' worth of gold. Tang recalls, "We came up with the idea by reading in the newspaper where a large cache of gold was found buried in Yugoslavia by wartime Germans. I remembered the famous German general Rommel's plight in Africa, so it just made sense to move the setting where we would have the Arabian sands to work with." Losing the male sidekick, Chan makes his journey with a Chinese contact (Carol Dodo Cheng), the long-lost granddaughter of one of the conspiring Germans (Eva Cobo De Garcia), and, midway through the film, a Japanese tagalong (Ikeda Shoko). As they make their way to the sands of

Eva Cobo De Garcia with Chan. (*Colin Geddes/Asian Eye. By permission of Media Asia Group. © STAR TV*)

the Sahara, Chan must contend with Cheng and Cobo's bickering, a pair of bumbling and greedy Middle Eastern characters, a band of thieves who try to sell the women as slaves and finally an army of mercenaries led by one of the original German soldiers. The wheelchair-bound soldier knows the location of the gold, but a key held by Chan and company is the only way to attain access.

Though the film begins to slump when the three reach the desert, *Armour of God II* contains some of Chan's best use of comedy. Critic Gerald Mast explains in *The Comic Mind* that "one way that film comedies communicate serious thought about human values is to stimulate audience reflection on the ironies, ambiguities, and inconsistencies presented in the comedy." Mast's theory best comes alive in a scene set inside an Arabian hotel. When Chan, Cheng, and Cobo turn in for the night, they find that their rooms have been ransacked. As the two women compete to coax Chan into staying in one of their rooms for the night as protection, two mercenaries enter the scenario with guns. Cheng (wrapped in a towel) and Chan try to alert Cobo of their situation, leading to a few innocent sexual innuendoes, but they are faced with a real threat. Both mercenaries have no problem handling Chan's fighting abilities. To distract the two, Chan flashes Cheng's body, makes jokes as to where the key is hidden, and when Cobo comes through for them, expands even further on a running sight gag with a gun.

Hong Kong ad for *Armour of God II: Operation Condor*. (*Colin Geddes/Asian Eye. By permission of Media Asia Group. © STAR TV*)

Armour of God II: Operation Finish the Movie

Jackie was carrying the entire film on his back, and it just got to be too much. He was complaining all the time and bored with all the stops that we had to make, even though he loved making the film itself."—Edward Tang

Chan encountered plenty of obstacles while filming *Armour of God II: Operation Condor.* Here are a few of the problems.

Chan directing *Armour of God II* in the Sahara. (*Courtesy of Edward Tang*)

1. Chan and the crew originally planned to shoot the entire film in Spain after his experience with *Wheels on Meals*. Without any scouting, they thought that they would find a lavish desert to double out for the Sahara. What they found instead was an expensive production house with no desert in sight. After wasting close to 2 million U.S. dollars, the crew ended up shooting only the beginning scene and the fantastic motorcycle stunt in Spain.

2. When the crew moved to Morocco, a simple scene in a village created one of the most unbelievable and unnecessary problems. Golden Way printed up hundreds of bills of prop money to be used in a market sequence. When many of the extras began to use the money (clearly printed with the Golden Way logo) off the set as currency, the Moroccan government arrested the production manager for distribution of counterfeit money to its citizens. She was held in custody for three months even after they had moved from Morocco to the Sahara.

3. Shooting in the Sahara, Chan had to stay an extra two months due to the countless illnesses endured by more than fifty crew members.

4. The actual part of the desert at which the crew was shooting was over twelve hours away from the nearest city, Casablanca. The lab at which the film had to be dropped off was even farther: Madrid. "We had to send people twice a week for supplies, and many times they would get lost and not return for days," remembers Edward Tang.

5. Hong Kong productions are known for having all of the editing and supposed postproduction work done right there while the film is still shooting. Since this couldn't be done in the desert, cans of film were delivered every two days to the Madrid production house for safekeeping. "We shot every day of the week except for Sundays, and yet we couldn't see what we were shooting. I can't believe the film turned out as good as it did," states Tang. After the crew returned to Hong Kong and struck a work print, two of the cans of film turned up missing. A week later they were mysteriously found at the Madrid processing lab.

6. Chan became so infuriated with the production that he finally decided to move the entire thing back to Hong Kong. Ten tons of sand had to be transported from the Sahara to Hong Kong to shoot the hotel scene and parts of the finale.

7. Over a million dollars was spent on the gigantic propeller in the wind tunnel sequence. It was so heavy that it would break off as soon as it was turned. Wires had to be situated to make the shot work.

8. Through all the transportation and other logistical problems, the film was shot in Hong Kong, Spain, Morocco, the Philippines, and Austria—when it only needed two locations!

The film grossed only HK $39 million, but it more than made its money back around the world.

At one point, each woman holds either the clip or the gun itself, but never both at the same time. Chan's juggling act with the gun is yet another lesson in patient timing. While the two men are busy fighting with Chan and trying to recover the key, the momentum builds with the same kind of rhythm used in his fight sequences. Even those two Middle Eastern characters are worked into the scene's dynamic.

When Chan, Cheng, and Cobo are all together, one can watch their chemistry unfold in almost the same way that Chan, Sammo Hung, and Yuen Biao operated during the eighties. Cheng is known for her comedy in Hong Kong and brings this attribute to her long-running talk show.

While situational comic exploits like this are genuinely pleasing, Chan begins to force humorous touches that don't quite work. Most Hong Kong films break out in song somewhere, stemming from the fact that so many stars are also pop singers. Chan, thankfully, doesn't do this, but for some reason in *Armour of God II* he takes a chance with a grueling three-minute tune set to a montage of travel sequences. A corny sight gag with a scorpion doesn't really work, either, and it becomes quite apparent that Chan's uneasiness with the shoot is showing through in his overacting. The camaraderie generated by the women, however, creates a nice touch of humor when the three engage one of the mercenaries, a sequence broken into three short segments.

While the women have their fun, Chan performs some of his greatest physical feats inside an underground bunker, with all kinds of levels, mechanical devices, and plenty of fighters getting into the mix. After the amazing motorcycle jump in the first third of the film, the bunker provides the setting for two incredible set pieces. The first is a large generator made up of three teetering panels. Chan and three of his foes must try to keep their balance while trying to fight each other. Shot from a tricky vantage point, Chan almost gets his head wedged between two of the panels.

The best is saved for last, when Chan is caught inside of a gigantic wind tunnel. The

(By permission of Media Asia Group. © STAR TV)

coordination of the fight that ensues shifts in relation to the direction and strength of the wind, bags of gold bars, and the temperaments (or operator skills) of the women who are at the controls. "Jackie has always had the idea of a fight inside of a wind tunnel ever since he visited a Mitsubishi car testing center in Japan that had a smaller version. Whether it was accurate or not, the only way I could work it in was to add a couple of German bomber planes," explains Edward Tang (only one bomber appears). The probability or the actual use of a wind tunnel this size is not important, because the scene is so amazing to watch. Chan has almost always stayed clear of using wires and other effects in his films, but the scene flawlessly uses both, the latter being a few miniatures at the end.

This film stood as Chan's opportunity to balance large-scale stunts and his normal fighting. The Indiana Jones series is quite apparent as the inspiration for *Armour of God II*, which uses booby traps, lethargic villains, and those everloving Germans, but Chan's style still reigns supreme in comparison. It holds up even today as well as a big-budget film, though it only cost 15 million American dollars, a paltry sum compared to Hollywood's standard.

Even with the sight gags, amazing stunts, and overall look of the film, *Armour of God II* will always be known for its problems, just like its predecessor was known for Chan's near-fatal accident.

TWELVE

From Cult Hero to Mainstream Icon

During Jackie Chan's first tour of duty in America, in 1980 with *The Big Brawl*, audiences had no other choice but to compare him to Bruce Lee. Lee brought a fierce realism to fighting that the audience could easily identify. Because Chan was Chinese, he was immediately labeled a kung fu fighter, but when his comic approach started to show through, it created too much of a contradiction to Lee's. Chan was also young, only twenty-five, and his abilities as a director and a performer had not yet matured to the level that they would only six years later with *Police Story*. No one had the chance to see Chan's trademark use of props or dizzying fight sequences, so Bruce Lee was their only vantage point. While he became a household name all over the world, Jackie Chan had lost the American market, where he was considered a failed martial arts star.

But while Chan remained an unknown to the American mainstream, videophiles embraced him. It all started in 1985 when Ric Meyers wrote the book *From Bruce Lee to Ninjas: Martial Arts Movies*. Sure, martial arts magazines like *Martial Arts Movies* had introduced Chan to that audience as early as 1980, but that was irrelevant. The book had a few problems (confusing Yuen Kwai as Yuen Woo-ping's brother and misidentifying a half-page picture showing Lee strangling Chan in *Enter the Dragon*) and only covered Chan's films up to *Project A*, but Meyer's book was one of the first in English to accurately portray Chan and his art. Meyers also helmed *Martial Arts*

Chan after a hard day's work on *Mr. Nice Guy* (1997). (*Courtesy Golden Harvest*)

Movies Associates, a fanzine in which he discussed Chan in great detail.

Yet it wasn't until late 1988 that Meyers really got the word out. A British television series called "The Incredibly Strange Film Show" was churning out programs about the underbelly of cinema. Horror maestros like Hershall Gordon Lewis and George Romero would have their own shows, as did Mexican horror wrestling movies and early sexploitation flicks from the late fifties and early sixties. A disgruntled female employee of the show wanted to bring someone in who had more of an even taste, and Ric Meyers was her man. After a brief meeting, Meyers convinced Jonathan Ross (host of the show) and his crew to take a look at the Asian invasion, which included Godzilla, Japanese animation films, and Chinese kung fu films. Meyers quickly assembled a five-videotape tutorial on the pioneers of this invasion. After Ross's examination, Jackie Chan and New Wave director Tsui Hark were to have separate programs.

At the time Chan was in the middle of filming *Mr. Canton and Lady Rose,* and Ross and his crew were able to go to Hong Kong to meet with him. Golden Harvest also helped by supplying action footage from some of Chan's best films: *Winners & Sinners, Armour of God, Police Story II,* and *Project A.* An offshoot of the original program, "Son of the Incredibly Strange Film Show" aired an hour-long segment on Chan, and the show eventually played in America. Unsuspecting viewers had no choice but to be drawn into Chan's world. The segment was the first to show Chan's devastating injury from his tree fall in *Armour of God,* and when viewers saw that he just went right back to shooting only a month later, they were hooked. Never before had they seen someone who was willing to go to those lengths to entertain the audience.

When the same people who had marveled over Chuck Norris and Bruce Lee began searching for Chan's films, the bootleggers came out of the woodwork. They discovered that Hong Kong films were already subtitled in English because of Britain's rule at the time, saving them some

labor. Video bootleggers aren't exactly the brains behind creating fandom—they just feed it. "The bootleggers wouldn't have known that these movies existed if I hadn't started getting them from Hong Kong and disseminating them amongst my buddies in the comic industry, the book industry, the television industry, and the movie industry," said Meyers. Anyone who prides him- or herself as a film connoisseur will have to look further than the local video store— just as a wine connoisseur doesn't build a collection from the supermarket. By looking in the backs of genre magazines like *Starlog* and *Fangoria,* this new elect could find ads for Hong Kong films and Jackie Chan.

Hong Kong cinema fans like Tony Rayns, Tod Booth, and David Chute also began to write frequently about Chan's films since they played in local Chinese venues in New York, San Francisco, and elsewhere. It's amazing to think that all of Jackie Chan's films have played in the United States since *Drunken Master* (1978), and no one but the Chinese-Americans had known about it. In 1990 someone at Miramax, one of the few successful independent film companies, did know about it. At that point, Miramax offered Chan the opportunity to make a splash in America for a second time, but it meant splicing *Police Story* and its sequel into one film. Thankfully, Chan declined Miramax's proposed edit.

With the multitude of videotapes that began to float around, coupled with various film magazine articles and an official video release of Chan's *Police Story* under the name *Police Force,* people were finally starting to take notice of what he was all about. To capitalize on the revitalized interest in Hong Kong cinema and Jackie Chan, two Golden Harvest representatives, Tom Gray and Roberta Chow (Raymond Chow's daughter), set RIM Film Distributors in motion. Though its parent company was Golden Harvest, RIM began an intense marketing campaign to put Hong Kong films in major American theaters under the banner "Festival Hong Kong," with Jackie Chan as the headliner. While the festival approach seemed to work in most major cities, RIM tried to branch out too quickly without needed marketing support. Some cities would put on these festivals without previewing the films for critics or offering literature to explain what they would be seeing. After two weeks, with no media coverage, the films would vanish.

With showings like this, RIM opted to move to something more conventional: Jackie Chan Film Festivals. Soon New York, California, and Chicago were bombarded with Chan's action films, and it seemed impossible for anyone to miss out on the opportunity to see him. Golden Harvest, nervous about saturating the American market with their biggest moneymaker before his newer films came out, removed his films from circulation and disbanded RIM, leaving Roberta Chow to head up a small branch of Golden Harvest in Los Angeles. In 1994, Media Asia was founded to handle international distribution of all Golden Harvest's titles, including those of Bruce Lee and Jackie Chan (although they would begin producing their own films as well in competition with Golden Harvest). Golden Harvest was waiting for the right moment to cash in on their biggest star—that moment would be when all of America could see Chan at once.

(As a consequence, only Seasonal's *Snake in the Eagle's Shadow* and *Drunken Master* could be acquired for showings, and even then in limited distribution. America's Chinatown movie theaters have suffered since they could no longer show their biggest draw. Only a handful of Chinatown theaters exist in America now.)

In the meantime, Hong Kong film fandom spread like wildfire. Mavens of the cinema created fanzines to meet the growing interest. Soon publications like *Oriental Cinema, Asian Trash Cinema,* and *Hong Kong Film Connection* took over to educate greenhorns in America about Chan and his fellow film pioneers. All of a sudden, Chinese video stores had to start selling and renting to the untapped non-Asian market, which managed to support many of these stores even though the new films generally weren't that good. Ironically, the only films that were not subtitled in English were from Jackie Chan. However, Taiwan, whose third spoken language

is English, had subtitled versions dubbed in Mandarin for rent in Mandarin Chinese video stores. The major distribution companies, like Tai Seng and World Video, had to start greeting the phones in English since many of the callers would be ambitious American video store owners.

It was becoming apparent that Jackie Chan would eventually claim the market he thought he would never have, and Stanley Tong was just the man to do it. During RIM's more successful days in operation, the most popular Jackie Chan film among casual viewers—not diehard Hong Kong film fans—was *Police Story III: Supercop*. The film was so popular that RIM even cut together its own trailer to show alongside American film trailers. In 1993, *Supercop* was being shown in limited release three years before Miramax re-released it. It was only natural that Stanley Tong's *Rumble in the Bronx* would be Jackie Chan's return to America. "Like all of Jackie's films, *Rumble* was made with the Asian market in mind, but we hoped that the North American setting would help the American market. What we didn't know was that it was going to be a big hit," stated Roberta Chow, *Rumble*'s producer.

New Line Cinema picked up *Rumble* for distribution for $5 million dollars, and after thirteen minutes were excised from the running time (mostly Chinese dialogue sequences) and the film was dubbed, it was released in early 1996. Avid Hong Kong film fans may have panned it during its original release in Hong Kong and select American Chinese theaters in 1994, citing a lack of plot, but to American audiences the plotless action film was what movies were all about. *Rumble* took in $9.8 million its opening weekend (the number-one film that weekend) and topped out at over $30 million by the time the dust had settled.

With a fantastic trailer and a rigorous marketing campaign, Chan was able to secure spots on David Letterman's and Jay Leno's TV shows, but the most surprising coup was the Lifetime Achievement Award given to him at the 1995 MTV Movie Awards. Pop culture icon Quentin Tarantino presented the award, though it was doubtful that MTV really knew who Jackie Chan was, since these awards are given out almost as a joke: the following year MTV gave out the same award to Godzilla! Composed of Generation Xers, the crowd listened as their god delivered the award along with a few words of encouragement. "He is one of the best film-makers the world has ever known! He is one of the great physical comedians since sound came into film. If I could be any actor, I would have the life Jackie Chan has," said Tarantino. The crowd went crazy with this proclamation, and even the people who thought Jackie Chan was a fad had to reevaluate their own feelings for the man.

It's important to note that Hollywood circles are still restrictive when it comes to anything and anybody that doesn't represent White America. The current state of cinema has left minorities to wander aimlessly through television channels rather than the big screen. Only a select few have been able to rise above the stereotypes to get star roles. During the seventies, when Bruce Lee and Sonny Chiba were becoming popular amid the martial arts film explosion, African-Americans were carving a niche with blaxploitation films. Later they even combined the two genres, launching Jim Kelly, Ron Van Cleef, and others in rip-off films like *Black Belt Jones* and *The Black Dragon.*

Latino actors have also generally been in a rut, but Asian actors, particularly, have had to work within stereotypes and have been kept from being anything more. Only films with Asian themes have presented them with opportunities to play more than Chinese food takeout drivers or gang members who know martial arts. Films like *The Last Emperor* (1987) are far and few between. If anything could have been the cause for such stereotypes, it was the exploitation genres and kung fu films that left a bad taste in the mouths of mainstream America with their atrocious dubbing and weak production values. Bruce Lee was different because he was known in America before his Hong Kong film days, due to *The Green Hornet* television series, among others, during the sixties.

Jackie Chan still had to fight this system

even during the so-called politically correct nineties. For example, hours of photography were shot for the *Rumble in the Bronx* poster, yet a large fist was the only thing to make it on the original one sheet. Though Jackie Chan's name is printed in big letters across the top of the poster, all of the credits with Chinese names listed below are darkened to the point that one would have to be looking only inches away from the poster to be able to make them out. In the Americanization of Chan, his Hong Kong origins and ties would be downplayed. The film's dubbing made things even worse, but Chan at least looped his own voice.

The most surprising aspect of *Rumble in the Bronx* was its "R" rating. All of the violence was kept on a cartoonish level, and aside from a brief mooning, there wasn't any nudity in the film. Jackie Chan, Willie Chan, and Roberta Chow even went to the ratings board, pleading to have the rating changed to "PG-13." No go. The official reason for the "R" rating was the word *fuck* used in a sexual connotation, though it's doubtful that one would ever be able to hear this. "I think they [New Line] made some very judicious cuts," said Chow. Chan has always said that his films are family entertainment, and this was a slap in the face. Compared to most Hollywood films, an "R" rating for *Rumble* seems laughable.

Even with such problems, everyone knew who Jackie Chan was and what he was about. That was the point. New Line Cinema can be commended for pulling off one of the great marketing campaigns. A junket in several key cities also marked the film's opening—although the New Line representative who accompanied Chan had never seen one of his films aside from *Rumble!* As a direct result of this marketing campaign, the film's popularity continued on video store shelves.

Miramax picked up *Supercop* in a similar attempt to cash in on Chan's new U.S. popularity. By not doing their homework, though, Miramax released a film that was four years old in a market that had seen it countless times due to RIM's push two years earlier. Unlike *Rumble in the Bronx,* English-dubbed videocassettes of

Supercop had previously been made available by those same ambitious video store owners. The film would have done marginal business had it been released in August during its original time slot, but Miramax made the foolish mistake of putting it out in July. And what was so special about July—aside from the normal, big-budget Hollywood fare?

Carrying over from *Rumble in the Bronx, Supercop* still did tout Chan as the real thing who does all of his own stunts. Can you get any more real than the Olympics, going on at the same time? *Supercop* ended up making half of what *Rumble* did, and the dubbing actually called Chan "the Supercop," whereas the original makes mention of the subtitle only once (a scene ironically cut from the American version)! Chan and Michelle Yeoh did do their own dubbing for the film, which helped, but the soundtrack added vulgar raps and, even more idiotically, a redo of Carl Douglas's 1974 disco hit "Kung Fu Fighting."

While *Supercop*'s marketing campaign virtually fell apart after the film didn't fare well at the box office, Chan still appeared in television spots. *Entertainment Tonight* did an on-set visit, and *GQ* interviewed him during the shooting of his most recent effort, *Mr. Nice Guy.* Chan appeared again on David Letterman and Jay Leno.

But on this tour Michelle Yeoh would get in on the action as well. Managed by Terence Chang, manager of John Woo, Yeoh secured numerous television spots, such as with Conan O'Brien, Rosie O'Donnell, and *Entertainment Tonight.* Yeoh has a better understanding of English than

Chan, and America had an easier time accepting her. In a politically correct society, who says that a woman can't be an action star? Women embraced Yeoh, and Rosie O'Donnell's talk show was the perfect move. Yeoh mentioned that Chan didn't want her to perform the motorcycle stunt in *Supercop,* citing his belief that women shouldn't do action. Before the boos from the crowd could begin, Chan appeared. Originally, he was supposed to break a chair, but he let O'Donnell crash it over him instead—as if in repentance for his women and action comment. In any case, as a result of *Supercop,* Michelle Yeoh secured a Bond girl role in *Tomorrow Never Dies,* with Pierce Brosnan as 007.

Rumors flew in Hong Kong and Hollywood circles that Chan was emphatic about appearing alone on the public relations tour. Only a few autograph signings allowed Chan and Yeoh to be seen together. Both Michelle Yeoh and Stanley Tong had to find other means of earning the spotlight. Chan was also quoted on many occasions that he in fact directed a lot of *Rumble* and *Supercop,* which led to another rumor: that Chan and Tong would never work together again. The actuality is that Chan and Tong still discuss future projects, but Tong's success as an American filmmaker will have to take precedence.

New Line picked up *First Strike* (retitled *Jackie Chan's First Strike*), and it opened in America in January 1997. *Jackie Chan's First Strike* received more extensive cuts in its American release version—some twenty minutes—than did *Supercop* and *Rumble in the Bronx* in theirs. The first action scene comes along in ten minutes instead of twenty in the original version. The biggest cuts came in the underwater fight finale, where ten minutes of footage was trimmed, including the shots of the fake shark with feet hanging out his mouth. With other graphic violence cut from the film (characters killed by machine gun fire), *Jackie Chan's First Strike* was given a PG-13 rating, which helped introduce Chan to children. The English dubbing doesn't hurt the film too much (despite the fact that "Tsui" is pronounced every which way rather than the correct way: "Choy"), and Chan did his own dubbing again. Critical response was generally favorable. All in all, the American redo is a more satisfying film with its sped-up pace.

As Jackie Chan continued to establish his presence in America, the question arose over which—Hong Kong or Hollywood?—would be the bigger part of Chan's film future. One stirring rumor created a much publicized breakup between Jackie and Willie that never occurred. In theory, Willie Chan represents a part of Jackie Chan's persona—that part being the business side. Without Willie Chan, Jackie Chan would not be where he is today. As the story goes, an American agency went directly to Jackie to

express interest in representing him in the States. When Jackie reciprocated the interest, word got back to Willie, putting a strain on the relationship. It sounds like a soap opera, but it's entirely not true. Willie Chan set up meetings for Jackie Chan to get American representation, since Willie doesn't understand the way Hollywood works.

After much deliberation, Chan signed with the William Morris Agency, which represents many of Hollywood's top stars. They now represent Chan in the United States and the rest of the world except Hong Kong and South East Asia. When asked about this other representation, Willie Chan responded: "When you've worked with a guy for more than twenty years, the 'title' becomes rather unimportant! I only want the best for him. Suffice it to say, we are still working together." Willie Chan will always be managing director of Jackie & Willie Productions, and the two will continue to have a long, prosperous business future together.

Chan has had some recent shots at Hollywood film roles, but they weren't exactly what he was looking for. Chan was supposed to have starred alongside Michael Douglas in *Black Rain* (1988), alongside Sylvester Stallone in the never-made *Rambo IV,* and as the villain in *Demolition Man,* played by Wesley Snipes. *Confucius Brown* was to be a buddy picture pairing Chan and Wesley Snipes, but Snipes was booked through 1998. An advance marketing slide in some film theaters announced Chan starring with Chris Farley for *Hollywood Ninja,* but an overexcited Columbia Pictures employee must have jumped the gun, since Farley is really teamed up with Robin Shou, star of *Mortal Kombat.* As for reality, Chan said it best when he stated, "The only way you can be sure that I am connected with a movie is when it actually comes out."

Bringing his career full circle—after bouts with Stanley Tong and a host of other directors, a reteaming with Sammo Hung, and countless offers from Hollywood—Chan is back directing again. His next film, set to shoot in Africa, is another action adventure story, this time using the French Foreign Legion and Chan as a mer-

Heart of Dragon
- Won for Best Song
- Nominations: Jackie Chan for Best Actor, Sammo Hung's Stuntman Association for Best Action Design, Lam Man-yi nominated for Best Music

My Lucky Stars
- Sammo Hung's Stuntman Association nominated for Best Action Design

1987
Project A II
- Jackie Chan's Stuntman Association won for Best Action Design
- Cheung Yiu-chung nominated for Best Editing

Armour of God
- Jackie Chan's Stuntman Association nominated for Best Action Design

1988
Dragons Forever
- Sammo Hung's Stuntman Association nominated for Best Action Design

Police Story II
- Jackie Chan's Stuntman Association won for Best Action Design

1989
Mr. Canton & Lady Rose
- Jackie Chan's Stuntman Association won for Best Action Design
- Nominations: Jackie Chan for Best Actor, Cheung Yiu-chung for Best Editing, Eddie Ma nominated for Best Art Direction

1991
Armour of God II: Operation Condor
- Jackie Chan's Stuntman Association nominated for Best Action Design

1992
Supercop
- Nominations: Jackie Chan for Best Actor, Stanley Tong for Best Action Design

1994
Crime Story
- Cheung Yiu-chung won for Best Editing
- Nominations: Kirk Wong for Best Director, Jackie Chan for Best Actor[3], Jackie Chan's Stuntman Association nominated for Best Action Design

1995
Drunken Master II
- Lau Kar-leung, Jackie Chan's Stuntman Association won for Best Action Design
- Cheung Yiu-chung nominated for Best Editing

1996
Rumble in the Bronx
- Nominations: Best Picture, Jackie Chan for Best Actor, Anita Mui for Best Actress, Francoise Yip for Best Supporting Actress, Cheung Yiu-chung for Best Editing, Stanley Tong and Jackie Chan for Best Action Design

Thunderbolt
- Sammo Hung Stuntman Association, Jackie Chan Stuntman Association nominated for Best Action Design

Mr. Nice Guy Script Excerpt

The following is an excerpt (in translation) from the script of *Mr. Nice Guy*, which opened in Hong Kong on Chinese New Year 1997. Directed by Sammo Hung, this film (and this scene) clearly has his signature mix of brutal action and light humor—all in the tight confines of a van. Sammo set up this sequence, and the actions are kept quick and personal.

To set up the scene: Jackie is captured by the notorious Demons gang, who are also holding Jackie's girlfriend hostage in return for an incriminating video that supposedly shows Demons' gangleader (Richard Norton) killing a man. The intensity of the van situation is kept intact despite the humor of a bicyclist (Sammo Hung) who blunders into the scene. The shaking of the van, Chan's facial expressions, and his unexpected actions also contribute a lighter tone to the violent aspects. "At one point, this Demons gang member could not get the rhythm down in throwing a punch at Jackie, so Sammo just steps out of the director's chair, goes into the van,

---

[3] He won Best Actor award at the Taiwanese Golden Horse Awards for *Crime Story*.

27-1

第27場
時：日
景：客貨車/計程車/街道
人：Jackie，Victor，四名 Demons 成員，
　　騎單車者，司機

（客貨車內，Victor 以槍指著 Jackie 額頭，兩名 Demons
成員拳打腳踢 Jackie，Jackie 以雙手護著頭部）

Jackie：我女朋友喺邊呀？
　　　　Where's Miki ?...I don't care what you do with
　　　　me, let her go.

（Victor 說著搶過 Jackie 手上的錄影帶，以錄影帶敲
Jackie 的頭）

Victor ：（憤怒地）仆街...我叫咗你唔好報警，同我玩嘢，好彩
　　　　我醒目..
　　　　I told you...no cops.

　　　*　　　　　　*　　　　　　*

（此時，客貨車停在紅燈前，由於 Jackie 在車上被打，
從外看，客貨車不斷搖動）
（一名身穿單車服，頭戴防護帽及護目鏡的人騎著單
車，停在客貨車旁，一手搭著客貨車的扶手）
（騎單車者見客貨車搖動著，好奇的望望車，再望向駕
車的 Demons 手下）

騎單車者：有咩嘢呀嘛？
　　　　　Everything all right in there ?

Original script page from *Mr. Nice Guy*. (*Courtesy of Edward Tang*)

and shows him exactly how it's done," describes
Barrie Pattison, a reporter on the set.

Scene 27/Daytime

*Inside the van. Victor is holding a gun pointed at
Jackie's head. Two members of the Demons gang are
hitting and kicking Jackie violently. Jackie uses his
hands to cover his head.*

Jackie: Where's Miki?!? I don't care what you do with
me, but let her go!

*Victor grabs the videotape out of Jackie's hand and hits
him over the head with it.*

Victor: Damn you. How dare you report me to the
police! Do you want to play with me? I want to see
what you can do now. I told you—no cops!

*The van stops at a traffic light. From outside, people
can see the van swaying left and right as Jackie is getting pummeled. A bicycle rider happens to stop next to
the van at the red light. His hand rests against the van*

*to keep himself balanced. The rider feels the vibration of
the van's movements, and he looks a Demons member
right in the eye.*

Rider: Is everything all right in there?

Demons member: Just fine.

*At this moment, Jackie happens to be kicked and lands
near the driver. Jackie screams out for help to the bicyclist. But before he can finish saying "Help!", Chan is
pulled furiously to the back of the van by the Demons
gang.*

Rider: Hey—you—

One of the Demons pushes the rider away.

Demons member: You go to hell!

*A shot shows him falling off of his bike and on to the
ground.*

*Two of the Demons drag Jackie outside of the van for
more punishment. Victor lifts his leg and blocks the
doorway.*

Victor: Hold it!

Jackie is pulled back inside the van.

Victor: Let's keep him until we're sure this is the right
tape.

Jackie: That is the right tape! Now let Miki go!

Victor: Let's go back! *(talking to the driver)*

*Jackie is facing Victor's gun. He is thinking about how
to escape.*

Victor: If you're jerking us around, you and your girlfriend are both dead!

*The van stops at another light and the beaten up bicy-
clist pulls up next to the van again. This time he is cau-
tious, and keeps his distance.*

*Inside the van, Jackie is sitting back to back against the
driver's seat. His hands accidentally touch the emergency brake handle.*

When the light turns green, the van starts to move.

Jackie suddenly jerks the emergency brake handle.

Everyone loses their balance inside the van. Jackie pulls the seat adjustment lever. He causes the Demon's member sitting at the front passenger seat to fall back. Jackie hits him as he falls backward. Fighting starts between Jackie and all the other Demons members.

The driver tried to keep the van under control, but he was knocked off balance because of the fight sending the van to run up on the sidewalk.

As the van begins to slow down, everyone bails out.

When the driver finally regains control of the van, the bicycle rider holds up a baseball bat that fell out of the van. He smashes the windshield shocking the driver in the process. The van loses control and hits a light pole.

The bicyclist shouts out with great joy. He carries his busted up bicycle and exits the scene.

Inside the van, Jackie grabs Victor, opens the door quickly and together they fall out. All other Demons members are trying to catch up with them.

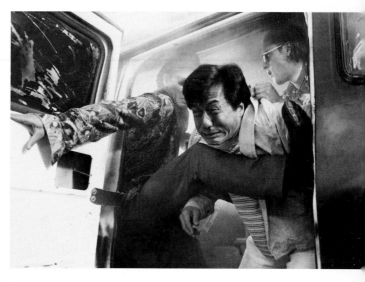

(*Courtesy of Golden Harvest*)

Finding Hong Kong Videos and Understanding Chinese Names and Characters

Although most of Jackie Chan's films will eventually make their way to local, mainstream video outlets, you do not have to sit idly by waiting for the rare risk-taking American distributor to release his films for mass audiences. More than 95% of all Hong Kong films are subtitled in English, and there are many Asian video stores across the United States that carry these films. Exploring the world of Hong Kong cinema can be a fun and exciting challenge—much like Chan's quest to find the "armour of god"—but it will also be hard work. Locating a specific film in an Asian store will not be as easy as just walking into an English-speaking video store and being able to find the video sitting on a shelf, nor will you be able to ask the clerk, "Where can I find *Thunderbolt* with Jackie Chan?" Locating these films is going to require a basic knowledge of the two main Chinese languages: Cantonese and Mandarin. This section will provide the basic information needed to locate Hong Kong videos for those who want their Jackie right now!

The first step is finding an Asian video store.

Most areas with large Asian populations will usually have primarily Asian shopping districts, and there will most likely be an Asian video store in these areas. If not, some Asian supermarkets carry laser discs, and try any place that promotes karoke. While Vietnamese, Korean, and Japanese stores are good places to search, the main avenues for finding these films are Cantonese and Mandarin video stores. The main differences between Cantonese and Mandarin video stores that will affect your search for Hong Kong films is the pronunciation of their spoken languages and the speed with which the various outlets are able to get recent Hong Kong releases.

Cantonese video stores generally have professionally recorded films from major distributors like Tai Seng and World Video, both of which are American companies. While these two companies also produce Mandarin-dubbed versions, Taiwanese-owned Mandarin stores often rent bootleg tapes made in Taiwan. The quality varies, but bootlegged Mandarin-dubbed versions of films are sometimes available on video months before the Cantonese versions. In some instances, if a film is released first in Taiwan, its Mandarin-dubbed video bootlegs may become available in the United States before the film actually opens in theaters in Hong Kong. An example would be the film *Wing Chun*, directed by Yuen Woo-ping and starring Michelle Yeoh. The film opened first in Taiwan, and Mandarin-dubbed tapes surfaced in America two months before it was released in Hong Kong.

When searching for videos in these stores, it is going to be important to have a basic understanding

English Name	Chinese Characters	Other Names (C) Cantonese, (M) Mandarin, (R) Real name
Jackie Chan	成龍	Sing Lung (C), Cheng Long (M)
Chan Yuen Lung	陳元龍	Chen Yuan Long (M)
Jackie's Stunt Team	成家班	Sing Kar Pan (C), Chen Jia Ban (M)
Ng See-yuen	吳思達	Wu Si-yuan (M)
Hwang Jang-lee	黃正利	Wong Ching-lai (C), Huang Jheng-li (M)
Yuen Woo-ping	袁和平	Yuan He-ping (M)
Simon Yuen	袁小田	Yuen Siu-tin (C), Yuan Xiao-tian (M)
Sammo Hung	洪金寶	Hung Kam-bo (C), Hong Jin-bao (M)
Yuen Biao	元彪	Hsia Ling-jun (R), Yuen Biu (C)
Yuen Wah	元華	Yuan Hwa (M)
Yuen Kwai	元奎	Yuen Fuei (C), Yuan Kui (M)
Fong Hak-on	馮克安	Fang Ke-an (M)
Mars	火星	Fwa Sing (C), Huo Xing (M)
Kenneth Low	盧惠光	Low Houi-kang (R), Lo Wai-kwong (C), Lu Hui-guang (M)
Stanley Tong	唐季禮	Tong Kwai-lai (C), Tang Ji-li (M)
Lau Kar-leung	劉家良	Liu Jia-liang (M)
Michelle Yeoh	楊紫環	Yeoh Choo-kheng (R), Yeung Chi-king (C), Yang Zi-huan (M)
Maggie Cheung	張曼玉	Cheung Man-yok (C), Zhang Man-yu (M)
Anita Mui	梅艷芳	Mui Yim-fong (C), Mei Yan-fang (M)
Dick Wei	狄威	Ti Wei (C), Di Wei (M)
Whang Inn-sik	黃仁植	Wong Yan-jek (C), Huang Ren-zhi (M)
James Tien	田俊	Tien Juan (C), Tian Juan (M)
Directing	導演	
Starring	領銜主演	
Action directing/ Fight choreography	武術指導	

新精武門 *New Fist of Fury*

少林寺木人拳 *Shaolin Wooden Men*

蛇鶴步 *Snake and Crane Arts of Shaolin*

劍、花、煙雨、江南 *The Killer Meteors*

成龍拳 *To Kill with Intrigue*

飛渡捲雲山 *Magnificent Bodyguards*

一招半式闖江湖 *Half a Loaf of Kung Fu*

蛇形刁手 *Snake in the Eagle's Shadow*

拳精 *Spiritual Kung Fu*

龍拳 *Dragon Fist*

醉拳 *Drunken Master*

笑拳怪招 *The Fearless Hyena*

迷你特攻隊 *Fantasy Mission Force*

師弟出馬 *Young Master*

殺手壕 *The Big Brawl*

砲彈飛車 *Cannonball Run*

龍少爺 *Dragon Lord*

奇謀妙計五福星 *Winners & Sinners*

砲彈飛車 II *Cannonball Run II*

A計劃 *Project A*

快餐車 *Wheels on Meals*

福星高照 *My Lucky Stars*

夏日福星 *Twinkle, Twinkle Lucky Stars*

龍的心 *Heart of Dragon*

威龍猛採 *The Protector*

警察故事 *Police Story*

龍兄虎弟 *Armour of God*

A計劃續集 *Project A II*

飛龍猛將 *Dragons Forever*

警察故事續集 *Police Story II*

奇蹟 *Mr. Canton and Lady Rose*

飛鷹計劃 *Armour of God II: Operation Condor*

火燒島 *Island of Fire*

雙龍會 *Twin Dragons*

警察故事III超級警察 *Police Story III: Supercop*

城市獵人 *City Hunter*

重案組 *Crime Story*

醉拳 II *Drunken Master II*

紅番區 *Rumble in the Bronx*

霹靂火 *Thunderbolt*

警察故事4簡單任務 *Police Story IV: First Strike*

一個好人 *Mr. Nice Guy*

狩獵大冒險 *Who Am I?*

of Cantonese and Mandarin. This is because most of the films in an Asian video store will not have box covers, although the title and stars' names will usually be listed on the actual tape. As mentioned earlier, Cantonese is the main variety of Chinese spoken in Hong Kong, although that will change with the country's reunification with Mainland China. Mandarin is the most widely used variety of Chinese spoken in Mainland China and is also spoken in other parts of Asia, such as Taiwan; it even has different dialects.

While Cantonese and Mandarin have two different spoken languages, Cantonese uses Mandarin written characters, so these are universally understandable. For example, someone who speaks Cantonese but not Mandarin and someone who speaks Mandarin but not Cantonese would be able to communicate with each other through written language even though their spoken languages differ. This becomes important to your video search when you realize that Jackie Chan's name in Cantonese is Sing Lung, but the Mandarin translation is Chen Long. Both names sound different when spoken and are spelled differently in English; but as long as you know what the Chinese characters for Jackie Chan are, you will be able to find his films in either a Cantonese or Mandarin video store. Similarly, the English name of Chan's costar in *Police Story* is Brigitte Lin. Her name in Cantonese is Lam Ching-ha and in Mandarin is Lin Chin-hsia, but the written characters for her name are exactly the same.

Another interesting fact about Chinese names is that the family name comes first as a show of respect. The first character represents the family name, while the second or third characters represent what would be the individual's "first" name. (A Western version of the Chinese name uses a hyphen to show that these second and third characters form the first name—so the hyphen in Sammo Hung Kam-bo shows that "Kam-bo" is his first name.) Let's examine the name Yuen using the characters in this section. In Yuen Woo-ping, Yuen is the family name shared by all the brothers and the father. Notice the characters. In Yuen Biao, the character for Yuen is not really a family name but a stage family name derived from the name of Master Yu Jim-yuen. So the character is different. Jackie Chan's Peking Opera name uses his original family name of Chan, followed by his stage name of Yuen Lung. But what about Ng See-yuen? The third character is different from both of the other Yuens because that is part of his first name. As a show of respect for his family an acquaintance would address him as Mr. Ng, but a close friend would call him See-yuen.

The characters in this section represent only a portion of the names of people discussed in this book. However, it should serve well as a basic reference for locating specific Hong Kong films in an Asian video store. All of the people listed have made many great contributions to Hong Kong cinema in addition to their work with Jackie Chan. Sammo Hung's resume more than doubles Chan's, and even Hwang Jang-lee can be found in close to forty films.

Also, the English titles for Hong Kong films are usually afterthoughts and are rarely exact translations. For example, the literal translation of the Chinese characters for the film with the English title *Armour of God* would be *Dragon Elder Brother, Tiger Younger Brother,* so knowing the characters for the titles of films can come in quite handy. Being acquainted with these characters will enable you to find a Hong Kong treasure of your own.

Martial Arts Glossary

bak-sing choy-li-fut A combination of the northern and southern fighting styles, it uses both long and short arm movements as well as kicking, punching, elbows, and backfists. It was used by Chan in *Drunken Master II,* along with his playful breakdancing, to lighten the blows.

drunken style Mimicking the ways of a drunkard, the proponent sways back and forth to keep his or her opponent on guard. The style employs what is commonly referred to as an "ox strike" or "crane" technique, which resembles holding a cup. Like many other kung fu systems, drunken style is often paired with others to increase its effectiveness. In *Drunken Master,* Chan goes through a particularly difficult drunken style known as the "Eight Drunken Fairies," which was created by an eagle claw master.

eagle claw Northern style of kung fu, also known as Ying Jow Pai, emulates the movements of a bird with long open hand strikes. Hwang Jang-lee used the style in *Snake in the Eagle's Shadow.*

hapkido Korean martial arts style that includes kicking and punching as well as throws and joint locks. Karate, judo, and aikido are essentially combined to make the "comprehensive" martial arts fighting style. Jackie Chan still studies this style under his current master, and Master Whang Inn-sik shows off his skills in *Young Master* and *Dragon Lord.*

hung gar One of five southern styles of kung fu taught in the shaolin temple, it was used by the real Hwang Fei-hung. As a descendent, Lau Kar-leung is one of the style's leading practitioners using it in *Drunken Master II* as well as his famous Shaw Brothers films. The foundation for the style is the horse stance, which is said to be the "strength" for it lowers the person's center of gravity.

kata A practice form made up of a prescribed set of movements designed to teach technique. Too much reliance on katas and not enough on sparring has led to the deterioration of American martial arts.

kung fu Although the name has been associated with martial arts (and made popular in America with David Carradine's television show), it actually means skill or ability. The literal translation is *kung,* "energy," and *fu,* "time." Although many different styles exist, kung fu can be divided into northern and southern schools. The northern schools encompass more long-range fighting and kicking techniques while the southern schools rely on more hand movements for short and mid-range fighting (kicks are used as well). Another term generally accepted to describe what kung fu has been used for is *wu shu,* or *wu su,* meaning "martial arts," or "martial arts technique."

lion dance Put on to celebrate good fortune (such as during the Chinese New Year), the lion dance also displays the expertise of the martial artists working the lions. Typically, there are two people inside the lion: one in the front operating the mouth and eyes and one in the back wagging the tail (a more difficult task given the poor visibility). During the dance, the lion must make its way through a number of obstacles—small benches, platforms, tightropes—to reach a lettuce or cabbage head hanging from a rope. The lion operators must work in perfect synchronicity.

sawhorse Also known as a small bench, a sawhorse is a narrow wooden plank with two supporting legs nailed to each end. It is a common sight in China. In southern China, a martial arts form by the name of Ban Deng Shu was even developed to use sawhorses as weapons.

Shaolin The first Shaolin temple was reportedly built in A.D. 377, and the primary basis was for preaching and worship. In 527, a Buddhist monk from an Indian tribe came to the temple, and ultimately paved the way for the monks to learn martial arts. Many kung fu films are set in and around Shaolin temples because of the unique relationship the monks had to morality and spirituality with hand-to-hand combat. The film *Master of Zen* (1992), directed by Brandy Yuen, focuses on the Indian monk who brought kung fu to the Shaolin monks.

tae kwon do Literally meaning "the art of kicking and punching," this Korean fighting style has become the most popular style in North America. Unfortunately, it has been watered down in America from the original version, which closely resembles hapkido. While the blocking mechanisms are poor, the style relies on varied, powerful kicking techniques. Hwang Jang-lee uses tae kwon do in *Drunken Master*.

Thai kickboxing A deadly style of kickboxing that remains active today in Thailand, former champion Kenneth Low Houi-kang uses the art's skills in his films with Chan. What separates Thai kickboxing from American kickboxing is the pain threshold for which the average career for a Thai kickboxer lasts only a couple of years due to injury.

Jackie Chan and Hong Kong Cinema Sources

JACKIE CHAN FAN CLUBS

Jackie Chan International Fan Club
145 Waterloo Road
Kowloon, Hong Kong
www.jackiechan.com
The Jackie Chan International Fan Club is run by Willie Chan and his assistant Davis Fung. This club gives its readers a slick, color thirty-or-so-page magazine filled with pictures, as well as film, biographical, and other information. Postage rates vary by country so one might want to try reaching them by fax at (852) 2338-7742.

Jackie Chan Fan Club USA
P.O. Box 2281
Portland, Oregon 97208 USA
ChanFansUS@aol.com
The US fan club sends out a monthly newsletter chronicling Chan's activities, and encloses an order form for movie posters and other memorabilia. Club members are alerted about Chan's US appearances so that they have opportunities to see him in person.

Australian Jackie Chan Fan Club
P.O. Box 795
Gladesville, NSW 2111
Australia

Jackie Chan United Kingdom Fan Club
P.O. Box 1989
Bath, BA2 2YE
United Kingdom

The Canadian Jackie Chan Fan Club
3007 Kingston Road
Box 109
Scarborough, Ontario
Canada M1M 1P1

FANZINES

Asian Eye
253 College Street #108
Toronto, Ontario, M5T 1R5, Canada
Covers all areas of Asian cinema sans personal comment. The fanzine's main advantage is its origin, since many Hong Kong film stars and directors live in Canada.

JACKIE CHAN: INSIDE THE DRAGON

Cineraider
P.O. Box 240226
Honolulu, Hawaii 96824-0226
For those who want their information laced with the latest gossip, look no further than this very enjoyable, intelligently written fanzine from Hawaii. Chinese characters are listed with many of the films that are reviewed.

Eastern Heroes
3a Buck Street
Camden, London, NW1 8NJ, England
Covers only Hong Kong action films. The fanzine has started selling its own films dubbed in English for the European market, and they have frequent interviews with stars and directors. Naturally, they tend to talk about British stars who work in the Hong Kong cinema. Nevertheless, the information is excellent.

Hong Kong Film Connection
P.O. Box 867225
Plano, TX 75086-7225 USA
Editor-in-Chief, Clyde Gentry III
Covers the complete spectrum of Hong Kong cinema as well as Jackie Chan. It is not limited to just action films, but it is limited to Hong Kong cinema. The fanzine is self-published on slick paper and has frequent interviews with stars and directors. Chinese characters are placed next to the films in discussion.

BOOKS

The Essential Guide To Hong Kong Movies, Rick Baker and Toby Russel, Made in Hong Kong, 1994.
From Bruce Lee to the Ninjas: Martial Arts Movies, Ric Meyers, Citadel Press 1984.
Hong Kong Action Cinema, Bey Logan, Overlook Press, 1996.
Sex and Zen & A Bullet in the Head, Stefan Hammond and Mike Wilkins, Fireside/Simon and Schuster, 1996.

VIDEO

Facets Video
1517 West Fullerton Avenue
Chicago, Illinois 60614
1-800-331-6197
sales@facets.org
Special Hong Kong action and Asian video catalogs in addition to its regular catalog.

Far East Flix
5913 68th Avenue
Ridgewood, NY 11385
Send three dollars for their catalog.

Tai Seng
170 Spruce Avenue
Suite 200
South San Francisco, California 94080
415-871-8118
www.taiseng.com
US distributor of Hong Kong videos. Catalog available.

World Video and Supply Inc.
150 Executive Park Boulevard
Suite 1600
San Francisco, California 94134
415-468-6218
US distributor of Hong Kong videos.

CYBER SITES

Many have sprung up—either for Chan, specific films, or Hong Kong films in general. Browsing for "Chan" or a specific film title (especially one picked up by for U.S. distribution) will always turn up something interesting. Here are a select few:

Jackie Chan International Fan Club
www.jackiechan.com

Jackie Chan Fan Club USA
www.spiritone.com/~chanfans

Drunken Master Homepage
shell.idtnet/~bellap

Hong Kong Movies Homepage
www.mdstud.chalmers.se/hkmovie/
Special section on Chan. Good place to start for information on Hong Kong movies.

Martial Arts Sources

The Original Martial Arts Encyclopedia (Tradition-History-Pioneers), John Corcoran and Emil Farkas, Pro-Action Publishing, 1993.
Great quick reference book for all styles and forms of martial arts with biographies galore on some of the best martial artists around. Chan is featured (but the filmography given is inaccurate).

King of the Ring, Benny "The Jet" Urquidez, Pro-Action Publishing, 1995.
Fantastic guide for learning the do's and don'ts of training either for health and/or competition. Urquidez covers all the different uses for bags, building hand-eye coordination on the speed bag, and teaches how to properly wrap hands.

The Martial Arts Explorer, CD-ROM, Soft Key Multi-Media Inc., 1995.
Interactive CD-ROM that gives the user a plethora of information on martial arts including philosophies, styles, and techniques on everything from Chinese Kung Fu to some of the Middle Eastern styles. It doesn't stop there since it has an actual moving video showing a master performing the techniques from each style. For less than thirty dollars, it's a godsend for martial arts enthusiasts.

References

Books and Periodicals
Altman, Rick. "A Semantic/Syntactic Approach." *Film Genre Reader*. Ed. Barry Keith Grant. Austin, Texas: University of Texas Press, 1986.

Dannen, Fredric. "Hong Kong Babylon." *The New Yorker*. August 7, 1995.

Garcia, Roger. "Yuen Woo-ping's Wong Fei Hong." *Hong Kong Film Magazine*. 1994, Number 3.

Geddes, Colin. "Smashing Through the Looking Glass." *Asian Eye*. Summer 1995, Number 2.

Ho, Sam. "Dissecting The Eagles Shooting Heroes." *Hong Kong Film Connection*. 1994, Volume II, Issue V.

Huen Jung-yun. "Superstar Jackie Chan." *Sing Tao Daily*. Series of articles. November 1–December 3, 1996.

Ingram, Bruce. "Fast-moving Jackie Chan's Slow on the Set." *Variety*. March 18, 1991.

Kracauer, Siegfried. *Theory of Film*. New York: Oxford University Press, 1960.

Lent, John A. *The Asian Film Industry*. Austin, Texas: University of Texas Press, 1990.

Logan, Bey. *Hong Kong Action Cinema*. London: Titan Books, 1995.

Mast, Gerald. *The Comic Mind: Comedy and the Movies*. Chicago: University of Chicago Press, 1973.

Various Authors. *Jacky Chan: His Privacy and Anecdotes*. Hong Kong: 1980.

Various Authors. *Jacky Chan: The Martial Artist*. Hong Kong: 1980.

Neupert, Richard, Editor. *Aesthetics of Film*. Austin, Texas: University of Texas Press, 1983.

Tyan, Shuh-lin. *How To Appreciate Chinese Opera*. China: Overseas Chinese Affairs, 1987.

Interviews
Jackie Chan by Barrie Pattison, Brisbane, Australia, September 1996. Portions previously published in *Hong Kong Film Connection*.

Jackie Chan by author, Joey O'Bryan, and Ricky Miller, Dallas, Texas, February 1996. Portions previously published in *Hong Kong Film Connection*.

Jackie Chan. Faxed correspondence with author, 1995. For *Hong Kong Film Connection*.

Marc Akerstream, telephone interview by author, August 1996.

Russell Cawthorne, telephone interview by author, September 1996.

Willie Chan. Faxed correspondence with author, spring, summer, and winter 1996.

Roberta Chow, telephone interview by author, July 1996.

Chua Lam, telephone interview by author, September 1996.

Gary Daniels, telephone interview by author, June 1996.

James Ha, telephone interview by Sam Ho, September 1996.

Rosamund Kwan by author and Sam Ho, San Antonio, Texas, December 1996.

Kenneth Low. Faxed correspondence with author. December 1995.

Mars by Mi Mi Lai, October 1996.

Ric Meyers, telephone interview by author July 1996.

Hal Needham, telephone interview by author, March 1996.

Richard Ng by author, San Antonio, Texas, December 1996.

Ng See-yuen, telephone interview by Sam Ho, May 1996.

Richard Norton, telephone interview by author, June 1996.

Cynthia Rothrock, telephone interview by author, August 1996.

Sammo Hung by author and Sam Ho, San Antonio, Texas, December 1996.

Shu Kei, telephone interview by author, July 1996.

Alan Sit, telephone interview by author, July 1996.

Tai Po, telephone interview by author, July 1996.

Edward Tang, telephone interviews by author, summer 1996.

Stanley Tong, telephone interviews by author, August and September 1996.

Benny "The Jet" Urquidez, telephone interview by author, July 1996.

Keith Vitali, telephone interview by author, October 1996.

Whang Inn-sik, telephone interview by author, September 1996.

Index

Note: Page numbers in *italics* indicate captions and illustrations. Main discussions of individuals and films are in **boldface** type. Film titles used are U.S.-release titles.